The Importance of Vowels in

Music Education

The Importance of Vowels in Music Education

By

Milena Petrovic

The Importance of Vowels in Music Education

authored by Milena Petrovic

ISBN: 978-1-905351-35-0

© 2017 Milena Petrovic

Published in Great Britain in 2017
by the International Music Education Research Centre (iMerc)
Department of Culture, Communication and Media
UCL Institute of Education
University College London
20, Bedford Way
London WC1H 0AL

cover design, typesetting, production and printing: Sonustech digital solutions

copy requests
http://copyrequests.imerc.org

British Library Cataloguing-in-Publication Data
A CIP record is available from the British Library

All rights reserved. Except for the quotation of short passages for the purposes of criticism or review, no part of this publication may be reproduced, stored in a retrieval system, or transmitted, in any form or by any means, electronic, mechanical, photocopying, recording or otherwise, without prior permission from the publisher.

Contents

Contents	7
List of figures	8
Introduction	11
Acoustical features of vowels	17
The origins of vowels and phonosemantics	31
Genetic origins of vowels	41
Vowel systems and musical scales and intervals	49
Vowels and absolute pitch	67
Vowels and emotions	77
Summary	92
References	97

List of figures

Figure 1. The song "Never again"   21

Figure 2. The song "Zaspala devojka drenku na korenku", Phryygian mode.   51

Figure 3. The song "Zaspala devojka drenku na korenku" harmonized by Mirecky.   51

Figure 4. Gradual downward melody reaches the octave range while pronouncing the long downward accent.   52

Figure 5. Repeated tone or two tones which are a second apart as the range for the short downward accent.   53

Figure 6. The range of third upward for the long upward accent.   53

Figure 7. Repeated tone or two tones which are a second apart as the interval range for the short upward accent.   53

Figure 8. Guido's Hymn "Sancte Johannes".   59

Figure 9. One phrase from Guido's Hymn in a nearly perfect mirror-form.   62

Figure 10. Ut queant laxis, the chant.   62

Introduction

The present study relates to sound and meaning on the one hand, and the origin of sound (language and music) on the other through a focus on vowels and their significance in musical education. What is presented below provides an overview of the use, nature and role of vowels in general, inside the field of musical education. Some scholars and researchers pose that music and language share a common ancestor (Wallin et al, 2000) and that language evolved out of music for the sake of a rational organization of human societies (Rousseau, 1781). Others assumed that music as a sound that is organized into socially accepted patterns' (Blacking, 1973), evolved out of primates' reproductive calls and that language was the first to become established (Darwin, 1871). Language is considered as relying on specific cognitive principles (Chomsky, 1957), but the principles that govern language seem to be specifically adapted for language and have little in common with general principles of thought or other apparatuses that might be attributed to the human mind (Bickerton, 2000: 158).

The first basic function of both language and music was to express emotive meaning through variations in the rhythm and intonation of the voice (intonation prosody). In both language and music, emotional excitement is expressed through fast, accelerating, and high-registered sound patterns: the first languages were sung, not spoken, expressing emotions, love, hate, and anger (Rousseau, 1781). Cry might be the first word and the origin of speech (Herder, 1989), while the first languages were singing-like and passionate, they (Rousseau, 1781) originated from half-musical expression (Jespersen, 1895) and were made of messages (Wray, 2013). Vowels are represented in crying, laughing, groaning, shouting and universal affects (such as ɑːh, ɔːh) (Lissa, 1977), and also in the pre-speech phase of babbling. Soundless syllables, such as dɑː, bɑː, or pɑː – which some authors determine as the first expression that a child makes in all languages (Jakobson and Halle, 1956: 37; Eimas, 1970) may present the evolutionary step in the language learning process which lead to phonological structure of language (Emmorey, 2002).

As far as we can tell, there is evidence in literature (von Helmholtz, 1954/1863; Nettl, 1956; Burns, 1999; Schneider, 2001; Honingh and Bod, 2011; Brown et al, 2013, 2014) that sound frequency, and consequently musical and non-musical pitch, is mapped on particularly sized frequency-steps in all known and recorded cultural contexts. These are used to consequently form various scales, some equally and some unequally "tempered". On the other hand, language is divided into phonemes, the basic phonological unit, just as music is composed of basic elements such as notes that are combined into higher-order structures (musical phrases and sentences, themes and topics). Therefore, there may be a musical grammar, and the similarity of the brain's response to some specific violations of syntax in both language and music (Arom, 2000). Infants show sensitivity to non native contrasts in sound categories both in language (Patel, 2008: 82) and in music (Soley and Hannon, 2010) which they appear to lose when they start to learn sounds of their native language (Patel, 2008). While the process of language learning starts with perceiving syllables in sequences (Saffran et al, 1996), the process of music learning begins with listening and singing sequences of native tonal patterns (Krumhansl, 2000; Huron, 2006).

The article is organized as follows: In chapter one, named *Acoustic features of vowels*, we briefly outline the major aspect of the physiology of the vocal instrument as an integral part of voice production and therefore vowels. Formants, as the resonances of the vocal tract, are extremely important for producing vowel sounds and relationships among formant frequencies are crucial for vowel recognition. A speech quality of vowels (a clear pitch and a rich harmonic structure) is impossible without a fundamental frequency. The perception of vowels also depends on timbre, articulation, tempo and duration.

Chapter two, named *The origins of vowels and phonosemantics*, points to a theory which states that every sound carries a certain meaning which evokes certain aspects of a concept named after the sound that is contained within the concept (Jespersen, 1922). This discussion deals with the origin of language and vowels, and thinks of language as a creator of musical expression. For the expression of vowel sounds and meanings, movement of the vocal tract is necessary. The size of mouth opening during pronunciation dictates the size of the referential object and there is correspondence between a feature of high frequency and the category of small size. Many researches pointed out relations between sound and the image of size, underlying the intercultural features of the frequency of the voice pitch of phonosemantics (or sound symbolism). It is not just the size of the mouth opening (and therefore the used vowels) that portrays the size of the referential objects, but some scholars have experienced colors with specific vowels.

It is difficult to determine when exactly each vowel appeared in the history of human communication, but what we know is that vowels have a key role in language evolution and generating the sound/sonority of syllables in both singing and speech. There are also the different evolutionary origins and linguistic functions of consonants, vowels and data telling us about consonants being more independent from melodic information of speech than vowels are. In close connection with the origin of vowels are *genetic origins of vowels*, which present a topic of chapter three. Genetic and linguistic diversity could be followed between population genetics and language typology. We may associate sound types with physiological factors and certain phonetic features with blood-groups (each blood type is featured by specific intonation and accentuation), as well as facial and brain anatomy (areas involved in language and speech), influenced by genes, with vowel quality.

In the chapter four - *Vowel systems and musical scales and intervals*, we shall especially concentrate on the possibility that a number of vowels correlate with the number of tones in a certain scale across cultures. As symmetry and roundness present phonological universals of each vowel system, the tonal center is the universal aspect of the majority of worldwide scales. The smallest unit of language is the vowel, whilst in music it is the musical interval, and the interval of an octave has been shown as being universal. There are studies about the interval size of the spoken word, so vowels have the crucial role in determining the pitches, their alteration and chromatics. That is the reason why in this chapter our attention has been dedicated to Guido d'Arezzo's hymn "Ut queant laxis", where every scale degree is vocalized on a single vowel which gives timbre color and melodic tendency to rise, fall or stay level. Symmetrically built hymn according to the used vowels brings the idea of perceived emotion which depends on placing vowels on a different scale degree.

There might be the assumption that Guido used strict frequencies for his initial scale syllables and that these frequencies differ significantly from those today falling within the A being 440 Hz. The talk about the chamber frequency is closely connected with the talk about absolute pitch, which originated as a feature of speech. Chapter five is titled *Vowels and absolute pitch*. Tone languages could be proof that music and language share the same origin due to AP being a process of phonemic categorization and giving verbal labels to pitches.

Findings that non-musicians could produce from memory the absolute pitches of self-selected pop songs (Levitin, 1994) suggest that latent absolute pitch memory may be a more widespread trait within the population than the traditional AP labeling ability. Results of a recent study suggest that relative pitch memory and the quality and degree of music-elicited emotions impact on latent AP memory (Jakubowski and Mullensiefen, 2013). There are other insights into the role of emotion in musical memory (Eschrich et al, 2008; Jancke, 2008) and the final chapter, chapter six - *Vowels and emotions*, concludes about the ability of language and music to express emotional meaning. Vowels, as the smallest emotional unit, make a sound, while consonants make the sense, or, the commonly believed assertion says that vowels are the emotion (the emotional content of the speech is shared through the vowel sounds, because they are free and open) and consonants are the intellect (because the meaning, as the intellectual component is carried through the consonants). This assumption might exist because accents tend to have more difference in their vowel qualities than in their consonants, and vowels can help one label a speaker based upon a regional difference, a social class or economic group. A vowel has a more dominant impact on the listener's impression than does a consonant, mainly because a vowel has a longer utterance time and a larger amplitude (Boku et al, 2012). Human listeners are accurate in decoding emotional meaning from vocal cues, more than from facial emotional recognition (Scherer, 1981; Ekman, 1982). The articulation of vowels systematically influences our feelings, because the facial muscles are active in the vowel articulation process, especially as it relates to non-lexical emotional utterances. Guido d'Arezzo seems to know about this, due to him deciding to put vowels on different tone pitches and as such to produce different emotions. The link between vowels, musical intervals and emotions is also being discussed (Blacking, 1973), as well as anatomic features, such as the lower positioned larynx (Fitch, 2000) that enables diversity of speech sounds and rich palette of formants (Lieberman, 1988). The relation between vowel identity and emotional state has been proved (Rummer and Schweppe, 2014).

Chapter 1

Acoustical features of vowels

Music and language understanding both require the listener to abstract over various kinds of information contained in the acoustic stream (Bergelson et al, 2013). When listening to and understanding the sentence, we primarily attend to the meaning and abstract over speaker, gender, volume, emotion, dialect, and other speaker and context specific variables. Similarly, when listening to a musical phrase, we focus on the melody and abstract over tempo, form, rhythm, meter, timbre, volume, emotion, register, etc. Vowels, as the important speech sounds, present the stable sound categories in perception (Francis et al, 2003): the mind maps acoustic variation onto stable internal sound categories.

The factors that have crucial consequences for speech and vowel expression are: (1) tongue position control of shaping the vocal tract; (2) lip area control; (3) length of the vocal tract, which shifts the maximal vowel space; (4) range of vibration of the vocal folds. Human vocal expression in speech requires large dimensional measurements of the neural activity, which is mapped into equally complex motoric gestures (Assaneo et al, 2013). It is equally well known that acoustic properties of vowels vary depending on the individual talker, the rate of speech, and the phonetic context in which the vowel occurs (Gay, 1978; Lindblom, 1963; Peterson and Barney, 1952; Shankweiler, Strange and Verbrugge, 1977). Each of these has been shown to influence listeners' perception (Ladefoged and Broadbent, 1957; Lindblom and Studdert-Kennedy, 1967).

Formants are resonances of the vocal tract, which is responsible for producing vowel sounds with their timbre determining its linguistic identity. Vowels in natural speech consist of many formants. Perceptually, vowels that are close in an acoustic space are heard as more similar than vowels which are further apart. The position of the first two formants is the most important and critical factor in determining vowel perception (Patel, 2008: 56). For example, the vowel (ɪ) when produced by male adults occupies a different region in formants space from those produced by an adult female or child. It can be due to the differences in vocal tract length, especially the length of the larynx (Fitch, 2000; 2002). All mammals produce sound in the same way, by using the laryngeal and vocal anatomy, they all have vocal tract and formants. In humans, around three months of age, the larynx gradually starts lowering, and it reaches its lowest position between the third and fourth year of life. With the lowered larynx humans create a rich palette of formants and wide phonetic repertoire, because the tongue is freely moving horizontally and vertically. Human speech demands control of the CNS, motoric control of the tongue, lips and jaw, while tongue movements modify formant frequencies and should be synchronized with the lips and larynx vibrations. The next level of speech control refers to hierarchical organization of speech segments (consonants and vowels) in the higher structures such as syllables, words and sentences. Due to the morphology of the vocal tract, vowel production, especially (ɪ) and (ʊ), is possible only for humans. Formants are linked to the length of the vocal tract and body size: the lowest fundamental frequency, the longest vocal folds.

By changing the shape of the vocal tract, the frequency of the formant is also changed. Each vowel has its own characteristic filter functions: high vowels have a low F1, while low vowels have a high F1; front vowels have a high F2, while back vowels have a low F2. Different formant values depend on the position of the jaw, lips and tongue (Yildirim et al, 2004). The position of the tongue body during vowel expression determines front, high or mid vowel: there are 4 distinct corners of articulatory vowel space, such as high front, high back, low front and low back, where the vertical dimension is tongue height, and the horizontal dimension is tongue backness. Perceived vowel quality is strongly correlated with the frequencies of the two or three lowest formants (Jenkins, 1987; Miller, 1989; Nearey, 1989, Strange, 1989). For vowels, the frequencies of the first two or three formants appear to be the dominant acoustic correlates (Syrdal and Gopal, 1986). The first formant corresponds to vowel openness – vowel height (vertical dimension), the second one to vowel frontness/backness (horizontal dimension) and the less important third formant corresponds to roundedness (lip position) and is important in some vowel distinctions, such as the (r) vowel in the name "bird" (Patel, 2008: 56). Relationships among the formant frequencies, rather than the individual formant frequencies, constitute the primary dimensions for vowel recognition (Syrdal and Gopal, 1986). Vocal formants help the ear to recognize a vowel sound as the same vowel, even though it is sounded at different pitches.

Vowels are classified on the combination of fundamental frequency and formant frequency (Disner, 1980) and vowels with similar qualities have similar formant ratios (Lloyd, 1890). Perceived vowel quality is correlated with the frequencies of the second and third lowest formants (Jenkins, 1987; Strange, 1989) and acoustic properties of vowels depend on the individual talker and phonetic context in which the vowel occurs (Lindblom, 1963). One phonetic feature that has been found to accompany vowels is "intrinsic Fo" or "intrinsic pitch", which presents the tendency for the high vowels (ɪ) and (ʊ) to have a higher fundamental frequency than the low vowels (ɑ) and (ɛ) (Meyer, 1896). This theory is abandoned due to discovery that formants are independent of voice pitch in humans and other mammals (Lieberman, 1988; Fitch, 1997). It is well known that front vowels such as (ɪ) have a low first formant (F1) and a high second formant (F2), whereas back vowels (ɒ) or (ʊ) have a high F1 and a low F2. In shoga, the Japanese mnemonic/iconic system for representing melodies, the vowels are correlated to melodic direction according to their F2 ordering: a succession of the vowel (ɪ) shows the highest frequency in

F2, and (ɒ) with a low F2 was most often accompanied by a succession of high and low pitch in melody (Hughes, 2000). In the same way, Alpine yodelers freely combine senseless syllables with successions of notes: in 118 out of 121 cases melody descends in (ɪ) to (ɒ/ɑ) succession, and in the 133 cases melody ascends in (ɒ/ɑ) to (ɪ) succession (Fenk-Oczlon and Fenk, 2005).

Here we can make a short digression by comparing the nonsense passages of yodeler songs and Serbian ancient folk songs, where the highest pitch coincides with the vowel (ɪ): as in songs from the Alpine regions of Austria, in Serbian songs named *ojkanje* (in the mountainous parts of Serbia) we can hear a characteristic "cry" at the end of each phrase (Golemovic, 2005: 127). I want to point out that the specific howling of wolves perhaps might be imitated by Serbs when creating their traditional type of singing (Petrovic and Ljubinkovic, 2011). The same, but less arbitrary and less demanding category, can be put songs without words, animal sound patterns and infant utterances (Nettl, 1956). And at this moment we can speak about the hypothesis that music is a precursor of language – a proto-language (Jespersen, 1894).

A well-preserved fossilized hyoid bone (three-year-old Australopithecus afarensis infant from Ethiopia, see Alemseged et al, 2006) shows a laryngeal air mask and laryngeal ventricles, like in all great apes and siamangs (Hewitt et el, 2002). Laryngeal ventricles are a generator of the sound source and help in producing loud and long calls (Hauser and Fitch, 2003). The spectrum of a vowel and the tone frequencies depend on the dimensions of ventricles (Kitzing and Sonesson, 1967: 479): the dimensions of the ventricles vary during speech, which is correlated with the vowel and the tone volume (Berg, 1955). However, the height of the laryngeal ventricle was at its minimum at lowest and highest pitches (Curry, 1937), despite ventricles might have an acoustic influence on the human voice (Flach, 1964). The increase in frequency of tone is accompanied by a systematic lengthening of the vocal folds (Hollien, 1960). During phonation, with increase in pitch, the laryngeal ventricle moves cranially (Keenan and Barrett, 1962) and increase in length when changing from respiration to phonation (Kitzing and Sonesson, 1967: 485). An interesting correlation is the finding that the dissonant coefficient for vowels (ɑ), (ɛ), (ɪ), (ɒ) and (ʊ), which were produced by a group of participants on different altitudes (200, 800 and 1400 meters), was decreasing with the altitude being increased. Therefore, the dissonant coefficient can be used as a hypoxia indicator (Milivojevic, 2010: 523).

The first main characteristic of vowel production is voicing. All voiced sounds have a fundamental frequency (f0), that is, the number of times the vocal folds vibrate per second. Fundamental frequency exists even in vowels spoken in isolation, giving to vowels a speech quality (Patel, 2008: 55, s. Sundberg, 1987). However, the acoustic structure of a vowel can vary depending on context (Lindblom, 1990) and it can be compared to the same tone that belongs to a chord in the harmonic progression. Namely, the same tone sounds different (higher or lower than its regular position) if put in a different chord with a different function in the harmonic progression. In the following example we can hear the four-bar intro of one famous Serbian pop song:

Nikad vise/Never again

Kornelije Kovac, composer
Spomenka Kovac, lyricist

Figure 1. The song "Never again"

As we can hear and see, there is a harmonic progression between the major supertonic (the second bar) and the minor subdominant (in the third bar). If someone tries to sing the melody in the upper system, they will come to understand a catch: it seems that a tone B (in the second bar) is a bit higher than the same tone (in the third bar). One may tell that the reason for the same tone sounding lower is because in the first bar we hear the B sharp tone as an altered tone. But, if we stick to the harmonic progression and sing the melody together with the harmonization, we can feel that the second B (at the beginning of the third bar in the upper voice) is lower due to the accompanied chord of a minor subdominant which appears after the major supertonic. This is an obvious example of how harmony influences intonation and how it can change an impression of tone pitch and its overtones.

Vowels are the most musical of speech sounds because they have a clear pitch and a rich harmonic structure. The vocal signal, as a complex periodic wave, is made up of several simple periodic waves and each of them is called a harmonic. The fundamental frequency is the first harmonic (H1), but there is a harmonic at each interval of the f0 up to infinity. Vocal fold vibration produces many harmonics above f0, all the way up to 5000 Hz in the adult human vocal tract (Patel, 2008: 55). Fundamental frequency (f0) is perceived by the ear as pitch. The f0 of the adult human voice ranges from 100-300 Hz. In addition to this fundamental frequency there are a theoretically infinite number of harmonics or overtones, or frequencies that are multiples of the fundamental frequency. A vowel involves harmonics when sounded at different frequencies. A mean fundamental frequency for male voices is 106 Hz (with a range from 77 to 482), and for female voices, the mean is 193 Hz (with a range from 137 to 634) (Stemple et al, 1995). However, when producing vowels and other voiced sounds, some of the overtone frequencies are louder or more prominent to our ears than others. It's as though the volume is turned up on frequencies within certain ranges. Harmonics dictate the personal character of our voice, and overtones give a voice a "dimensionality": "the second and fourth harmonics only add brilliance as they are merely octaves of the foundation tone (...) the third contributes a thickening of the tone, adding a certain hollow, throaty quality (...) the fifth adds a rich, horn-like quality and the sixth adds a delicate shrillness of nasal quality" (Jeans, 1937). It is very interesting to mention that vowel shapes affect the harmonic output: overtones will therefore be clearer with a group of matched vowels, with plenty of mouth resonance (as brighter vowels, harmonics are higher) (Jeans, 1937). In hearing overtones, the lowered larynx has a great role. Overtones must be the cause of the "vowelizing" of the tone sung: each vowel-sound is found to be due only to different overtones of the tone sung (Shaw, 1878: 51). When a vowel is sung, high or low, it is still the same vowel at a different pitch. In music, the same represents a chord in another key. Vowels are musical air-waves. Vowel-sounds are an exquisite musical harmony, being nothing but "chords" of the tone with its different overtones, different "chords" making different vowels. The musical scale is derived from a tone and its overtones. Vowels alone, like musical tones, will not make speech (Shaw, 1878: 51). One might say that vowels are the expression of pure harmonics whose precise sequence provides one of the most basic of cosmic laws. The harmonics produced by the vowel sounds provide the resonances that are able to affect various bodily centers (Leet, 1999: 179). One of the functions of the vowel sounds is to form the geometric angles that can separate out the harmonic tone with which it is in resonance from the tones of music or speech.

While in music overtones or harmonics refer to any resonant frequency above the fundamental frequency, in linguistics, vowel harmony facilitates the meaning and brings efficiency in speech. Vowel harmony refers to any type of long distance assimilatory process of vowels (sounds are separated by intervening segments – consonants) (van der Hulst and van der Weijer, 1995: 496). It is a type of assimilation which takes place when vowels come to share certain features with contrastive vowels elsewhere in a word or phrase (Crystal, 1992: 168). For example, in the Hungarian language there are fourteen vowels and vowel harmony exists:

words that have the high vowels in their last syllable reach the high vowels and vice versa (Vago, 1976). The vowel harmony is based on the opposition between high and low vowels. We may say that the root word reaches its suffixes, like a note when sung is not heard in isolation and the single tone sounds a whole chord of pure tones which are called harmonics or overtones. In the Serbian language we may see another situation. Root words are the main carrier of meaning. For example, to the word "rad" (work) different suffixes could be added, so we reach different words with different meaning: rad-nik (worker), rad-iti (to work), rad-ionica (the workshop), etc. All the words reached by adding the suffix to the root words make a word family. It is assumed that root words origins are from the Slavic protolanguage, similar to or borrowed from the other Slavic languages or Indo-European protolanguage. Some root words origins are onomatopoeic.

However, beside formants and the direction of formant movement (Nearey & Assmann, 1986) and fundamental frequency (Nearey, 1989), there are other factors that influence perception, including timbre, articulation (Lindblom, 1963) and vowel duration (Ainsworth, 1972).

Between each other, vowels differ in their timbre. In most languages, vowel contrasts are based on sonority and timbre (Trubetzkoy 1969: 69). As another universal, speech is based on organized timbral contrast (Patel, 2008: 51) of a vowel system which is achieved by vowels acquiring color from neighboring consonants (Cohn 1993; Clements and Osu 2003). Similarly, a vowel system can be contrastive for nasality only if there are output nasal consonants. Most of the sound energy is concentrated in vowels, while most of the linguistically significant information is concentrated in consonants (Harris, 2006: 1491). So we may hypothesize that sound belongs to vowels and meaning to consonant: as more voices are added and different vowels are introduced in polyphonic music, a changing mass of colors is received. Thus, vocal vowel color is in many ways tied directly to the independence of voices in music polyphony.

Articulation distinguishes different vowel sounds and determines vowel quality such as *height, backness* and *roundedness.* In high vowels, such as (ɪ), the tongue is positioned high in the mouth, whereas in low vowels, such as (ɑ), the tongue is positioned low in the mouth. According to the relative frequency of the first formant – the higher the F1 value, the lower (and more opened) the vowel, and opposite. The small percentage of world languages having only opened syllables (Blevins, 2004: 163), but all languages have low vowels (Bybee, 2001:191) and some variations in vowel quality that indicate contrasts in the vowel height dimension. Even if a language has only two phonologically contrastive vowels, the differences will always be in this dimension rather than the front-back dimension (Ladefoged and Maddieson, 1996: 286). Vowel backness presents the position of the tongue which is in the back of the mouth, during the articulation of a vowel (ʊ), and opposite during the articulation of a vowel (ɪ), the tongue is positioned forward in the mouth. According to the fundamental frequency, the higher F2 value, the vowel is at the front. There is a tendency for high tones to be sung on syllables with front vowels, while lower tones are to be sung on back vowels (Fenk-Oczlon and Fenk 2005). This may have a physiological basis, since we know it is easier to sing high tones with front vowels and low tones with back vowels (Nettl, 2000: 469). Roundedness refers to whether the lips are rounded or not – the higher the back vowel, the more intense the rounding.

It is important to remember that the articulatory configurations of vowels are due to control of the location and the area of one constriction that divides the vocal tract into one or two cavities, and to the inter-lip area. The vocal tract can be modeled by four cylindrical spaces: the back cavity, the constriction, the front cavity and the labial horn. For (ɪ) and (ɑ), this simplification can even be reduced to two tubes. The vowel (ɪ) can only be produced by controlling a palatal constriction at the front of the vocal tract, when F2 depends only on the remaining length (of the back cavity of the vocal tract), while F3 depends on the length of the constriction. To produce the first two resonances typical of (ɪ) can be generated by simply lowering the jaw. As the front cavity opens, a pharyngeal constriction is automatically produced. Front and back cavities are also necessary for a vowel (ʊ). The tongue position alone divides the tract into two cavities and the tongue and lip constrictions make the necks for these two resonances (Granat et al, 2007: 383).

In vowel systems, vowels are produced orally, but some languages, such as French, Polish or Portuguese, contrast nasal and oral vowels. Vowel systems are smaller than consonant systems, and a language never has more nasalized vowels than oral vowels (Ferguson, 1963). According to articulation phonemes and syllables can be produced slower or faster depending on perception of the final stop being voiced or voiceless: syllables with more phonemes tend to be longer than those with fewer phonemes (Klatt, 1976). The other reason for difference in speech tempo can be the tendency to speed up near the end of a sentence (Schegloff, 1982), similar to accelerating at the beginning of a music piece and slowing down the tempo of music at structural boundaries during playing, which may reflect principles of human physical movement (Kronman & Sundberg, 1987).

Speech tempo may be regarded as one of the components of prosody. The prosody is made of three traditional suprasegmentals of tone, length, and stress (Lehiste 1970, Kaye et al 1985). Stress is generally represented in abstract metrical terms (metrical stress), and many languages may have word *accent* and those in which accent is manifested as 'pitch' or 'stress'. There are languages that have no stress, but have tone. But, all languages have syllables, consisting of consonant and vowel (Greenberg, 1962:74) as the only universal model of the syllable (Jakobson and Halle 1956:37). The traditional division of languages between stress-timed and syllable-timed, proposed by Kenneth L. Pike (1945), dominated the phonological theory for almost half of a century. According to this dichotomy, certain languages, such as English or Russian, are characterized by stress isochrony, the phenomenon that stresses tend to occur at approximately even time intervals. The consequence of accentual isochrony is that unstressed syllables have to be reduced, in order to successfully be 'squeezed' into rhythmic groups. In syllable-timed languages, on the other hand, each syllable tends to take up an approximately equal amount of time, thus creating the impression of syllabic isochrony. The classical example of a syllable timed language is French.

So, the speech rhythm, according to its timing (individual), accentuation, grouping patterns, number of phonemes, vowels reduction, etc, is not isochronous, but the product of its linguistic structure (Pattel, 2008: 122). If we compared stressed syllables to their analogy to the basic beat in music (tactus in music, see Lerdahl and Jackendoff, 1983) it means that we always have to follow the scheme where stress in speech matches metric stress in music. But we all know that this kind of idealistic matching does not exist in real speech and music correlation due to non-isochronous of speech rhythm. In music, the meter presents periodic mental pattern, and some event is metrically prominent even if it coincides to metrically weak beat position, such as the case of syncopation. The body can produce regularity (with different body action) and poly-rhythm, but isochrony is only to be heard in speech (Petrovic, 2015). Because of the temporal irregularity of speech, the syncopation is almost impossible, just in rare cases of post-accentual length in the Serbian language (in the three-syllable words such as "de-voj-ka" (girl), "bes-kraj-no" (endlessly)). It seems that the ear ignores speech irregularities (Lehiste, 1977), maybe because the majority starts learning music and language on the base of the regular, periodical patterns made of meaningless rhymes or syllables. If infants discriminate languages only by the differences in their rhythmic classes (Nazzi et al, 1998), the rhythmic predictability might be associated to signaling phrase boundaries in speech (Lehiste, 1977). However, stress-based segmentation is found as universal (Cutler, 2000).

The other important feature of vowels is its duration, which depends on varying stress. Phonemic vowel length and speaking rate are two factors that affect vowel duration. In order to examine the influence of duration, researchers used isolated, synthetic vowels (Ainsworth, 1972). A particular acoustic correlate, such as shape of the spectrum, formant movements and duration, can influence vowel perception. While tonal contrasts are realized primarily by differences in fundamental frequency (f0) height or contour, they may also involve systematic differences in duration. The perception of duration, on the other hand, may be influenced by the f0 pattern. This type of interplay between tonal contrasts and duration is commonly reflected in the world's languages (Xu et al, 2007). Vowel duration tends to be inversely related to the approximate average f0: vowels on low tones are longer than those on high tones, while vowels on rising tones are longer than those on falling tones (Gandour, 1977), for example, in Mandarian language (Howie, 1976). In musical education, the speech rhythm, as the specific method for rhythmic reading, originated from the French numeric method. The author Galin was the first who investigated it, Cheve continued, and Aime Paris finally developed it into the form of the method. To notate the whole note, Paris used the vowel (ɑ), and for its division he used the vowels (ɑ) and (ɛ), while the tripartite division the author named with the vowels (ɑ) (ɛ) and (ɪ). To vowels the consonant (t) has been added, which is excluded if duration is longer.

A curious fact is that tone systems often correlate with non-tonal languages with length opposition. Lehiste (1976) found that listeners judge a dynamic (falling-rising or rising-falling), as opposed to a flat f0 pattern, to be longer even when the stimuli are of equal acoustic duration. From my educational practice, I met students who mix pitches and duration of the same repeated tones if there is an added dynamic, particularly crescendo. Brigner (1988) found that the duration of a pure tone high frequency was perceived to be longer than the duration of a low frequency tone. Height, that is specific for speech, makes the spoken phrase to be heard as convincingly as it is sung, by repeating the phrase several times over (Deutsch 2008: 8). Different expressive timing in music, which is completely individual in performers, has its relationship to prosodic speech structure, i.e. the same sentence spoken by different speakers will have a different temporal pattering of syllables and phonemes (Patel, 2008: 116). In a sample of thirty-four languages the mean number of syllables was around seven (Miller, 1956), from five in Dutch to ten in Japanese (Fenk-Oczlon and Fenk, 1999). In the seventy-five percent of the phrases in the Essen Folksong Collection (Huron, 1996; Temperley, 2001) contain from six to ten notes. Interestingly enough, a very short duration of our musical and linguistic phrases may coincide with the coos of Japanese macaques (Sugiura and Masataka, 1995). Thus, many parallels between language and music can be explained by perceptual and cognitive mechanisms involved in both speech and music. One of them is ponosemantics, presenting a word which suggests the *meaning* that comes from *sounds*. The first language that might have originated from the human need to imitate natural sounds by using onomatopoeia, mimicry and sound synesthesia – a word sounds similar to an image, the movement or an emotion of a referential object. But the older forms of words are onomatopoeic, which sound like the concept they describe (Petrovic, 2014c). Similarly, sound symbolism or phonosemantics means that every sound carries a certain meaning, which evokes certain aspects of a concept in whose name the sound is contained.

Chapter 2

The origins of vowels and phonosemantics

During the evolution of speech, vowels received referential meaning, which means that the sound of the less specialized tone-dominated precursor diminished (Brown, 2000). The formant structure of the vowels remains the same whether the respective syllables are spoken or sung. The phonosemantics present the universal tendency to use words which suggest the meaning that comes from vocal sounds or phonemes carry meaning in and of themselves, simulating acoustic cues carrying the melody of the speech (Meyer, 2007). A word has two components: word form (signifier) and meaning (signified). The sound of words evokes the concepts they refer to. Socrates proposed that there is a connection between the way a word sounds and its signifiers: the Greek letter *rho*, for him, expresses motion (Locke, Leibniz, Genette, Magnus, Jakobson, Jespersen, Firth, Sapir). In the same way, in the Serbian language, the sound (r) is used in a great number of verbs that indicates motion (*trčati/runing, raditi/working, graditi/building*) (Petrovic, 2014: 77). It is interesting to mention that Japanese cannot make a distinction between (r) and (l) sounds as phonemes (Goto, 1971), so we assume that it is difficult for them to sing a traditional Western European solfeggio scale (with Re and La solmization syllables).

Traditional people, those who have lived in a close contact with nature, used onomatopoeia to name living beings. The famous linguist Otto Jespersen established and studied sound synesthesia in the twenties of the 20th century. He believed that language was created from musical expression: the sound (I) refers to something small, while the sounds (ʊ) and (ɒ) to something big, due to the size of mouth opening during pronunciation. Therefore, vowels are the product of the physical movement of lips and the tongue, so the mimicry of the object's size has been achieved (Jespersen, 1922). In a wide range of cultures, high front vowels are perceived as small and denote small things, whereas low back vowels are perceived as big and denote large things (Ultan, 1978). Maybe that is the reason why the high front vowels (I) or (ɛ) are easier to be sung in high tones (Nettl, 1954). Correspondence between a feature of high frequency and the category of small size brings us to the universal phenomenon of sound symbolism or phonosemantics (Petrovic, 2014c: 437).

Among one hundred and thirty-six languages, diminutive sound symbolism is associated with marked phonological features - high and/or front vowels (Ultan, 1978). Diminutive is most often symbolized by high or high front vowels and high tone. Proximal distance is symbolized by front or high vowels: "high front vowels reflect higher second formant frequencies (...) the higher the tone, the higher the natural frequency (...) a correspondence between a feature of high frequency and the category of small size appears (Ultan, 1978: 545). In most words, the combination of the phonetic signifier with the semantic signified is arbitrary, and aspects such as large or little (not big or small) have phonetic and semantic features in the vowel. We are now getting into the field of metaphors which exist in language and music (Petrovic and Milankovic, 2013b). If the vowel (I) connotes the high (and therefore small) objects, then it seems understandable why it makes a part of a vocal syllable in a music scale Mi (the leading tone to Fa) and Si (the leading tone to the upper Do). The higher the place of articulation, the lower the formant frequency is: in the articulation of front vowels, the tongue occupies a much larger volume in the mouth than it does for back vowels (Ultan, 1978). Therefore, the frequency of the second formant (I) becomes high and (ʊ) low. But according to the first formant, (I) and (ʊ), and (ɛ), and (ɒ) are of equal height. Sound symbolism is reflected by different articulation and different formants of the speech signal. Beside the auditory phenomenon refers to the sole assessment of the overall output, articulatory gestures have a kinesthetic effect on how speech sound feels (Tsur, 2006: 921). Empirical works do suggest that pitch height is strongly associated with spatial verticality (Milankovic, Petrovic, Petrovic, 2003), but also, the higher pitches were generally positioned above and to the right of lower pitches positioned to the left-side (Stevens and Arieh, 2005). There are perceptual correlations between the pitch of sounds and their perceptual brightness, with high pitched sounds being rated as brighter than low pitched sounds (Hinton, Nichols, & Ohala, 1994; Nuckolls, 1999; Marks, 1996; Newman, 1933).

Many researchers have pointed out some existing relations between sounds and the image of size. It has been found that ninety-five percent of English-speaking adults associated the round shape with the pseudoword "bouba" and the spiky shape with "kiki" (Ramachandran & Hubbard, 2001). 2.5-year-old English-speaking children and adults significantly associated pseudo words containing rounded vowels to round shape and unrounded vowels to spiky shapes (Maurer, Pathman, & Mondloch, 2006). Jagged two dimensional objects were labeled as tough, strong, and unfriendly, whereas curved images were labeled as peaceful, relaxed, and quiet (Lindauer, 1990). English speakers tend to associate two nonce words (*mil* and *mal*) with two tables (small and large), and results show the vowel (ɑ) evokes a larger image than (ɪ) (Sapir, 1929). This idea has been proven in the following study (Ultan, 1978), while other researchers found that back vowels are perceived as larger than front vowels in English speakers (Newman, 1933). Some scholars have suggested that size-related sound symbolism is grounded on the size of the oral cavity (Berlin, 2006; Paget, 1930; Sapir, 1929), i.e. complex relationship between body-size, the size of articulatory organs and size of vibration (the frequency code underlies the symbolic use of voice pitch in sound, see Ohala, 1994).

The frequency of voice pitch of sound symbolism is intercultural, but presents a cross-species phenomenon, due to its great survival and evolutionary value both in mating and settling disputes: animals try to appear as large as possible by erecting hairs/feathers (Tsur, 2006). In examinations of ethnozoological literature, it has been shown that larger fish and birds were typically given names containing low back vowels while smaller fish and birds were typically given names containing high front vowels (Berlin, 1994). According to this study, in Huambisa (the North Central Peru language) there is a strong correlation between bird names and segments having high frequencies (F2). Results show the phonetic characteristics of the bird and fish names in Huambisa suggest the workings of universal sound-symbolic processes (Bettex & Demolin, 1998: 1337). This suggests that the sound symbolism coding of bird names is made in terms of high or low frequency, but also of temporal (timing) and intensity aspects (Petrovic, 2014b:278).

The F0 of voice though convey an impression of the size of the signaler, since F0 is inversely related to the mass of the vibrating membrane (vocal cords in mammals, syrinx in birds), which is correlated with overall body mass (Morton, 1977). The more massive the vibrating membrane, the more likely secondary vibrations could arise to an irregular or rough voice quality, which gives impression of an antagonist being large and dangerous. On the other side, being non-threatening is related to a tone-like vocalization (Tsur, 2006: 913). An animal produces rough and low frequency vocalization to give the impression of being large and dangerous. This cross-species F0-function correlation is called "the frequency code" (Ohala, 1994: 330). Low pitch sounds, presented as both pure tones and low back vowels, were strongly associated with large, heavy, slow, and masculine traits, while high tones and high front vowels were associated with smallness, lightness, femininity, and activity (Tarte, 1981).

According to some experiments where spontaneous speech was digitally processed, the results indicated that lower fundamental frequency does make a voice sounds more dominant (Ohala, 1994). Aggressive animals utter low-pitched harsh sounds, while appeasing animals use high-pitched, often tonal sounds (Morton, 1994: 350–353). However, the lowered larynx can be noticed in some deer species, in autumn, during the roar which precedes mating. While roaring, the larynx is lowering under the anatomic limits, so these species aim to have their size appear as enlarged by lowering the resonance of the vocal tract (Fitch, 2000). It is tempting to mention that the specific frequency of the male's roar induces female ovulation (Fitch, 2002). Varying the position of the larynx during vocalization, mammals can change the configuration of the vocal tract and create nasal and oral sounds as well as their combinations. The enlarged larynx is present in some ape species (genus alonatta) and those small animals create very low and deep sounds. In one bat species (hypsignathus monstrosus), the larynx is oversized, filling the whole thoracic hole. In male humans, larynx enlargement is typical for the puberty phase, when vocal tract becomes longer and the formant becomes lower (Titze, 1989; Fitch, 2002).

Anatomic features are related with voice/vowel color (timbre) and the produced emotion. Lomonosov, a well known Russian poet and scientist of the 18th century, applied idiosyncratic theory to his later poems, which explains that tender subjects need words containing the close front unrounded vowel (I) and close mid-front unrounded vowel (ɛ), whereas things that may cause fear need words with a close back rounded vowel (ʊ) and a close mid-back rounded vowel (ɒ). It may be called the early version of what is today called sound symbolism. Synesthesia sometimes goes parallel with stressed and initial vowels – the color of the word is linked to its stress (Simner, 2006: 281). The relationships between specific vowel phones and specific colors occupied researchers' attention. A close connection of the vowels (ɒ) and (ʊ) with the specifically darker colors, and (ɛ) and (I) has been investigated in comparison with the specifically brighter colors: the more colored vowels are associated with the more vivid colors, while the vowels (ʊ) and (I) even with the black-white range (Jakobson, 1962: 386). The other studies (Cytowic, 1989; Wheeler, 1920) show that the vowels (I) and (ɛ) tend to be white/yellow/bright, and (ɒ) tends to be black and/or white. The vowel (ɛ) is often seen as yellow, (ɑ) as red, "high" vowels as being brighter/whiter, and low vowels darker/blacker: the order of vowels from darkest to brightest looks as follows: (ʊ), (ɒ), (a, (ɛ), (ɪ) (Marks, 1978: 86-89). Between the period of 1820 and 1870 the vowels color has had huge interest in European literature: in one verse of Rimbaud's *Vowels* (1871) (a) is black, (ɛ) is white, (ɪ) is red, (ʊ) is green, (ɒ) is blue, while Hugo wrote that (a) and (ɪ) are white and bright, while (ʊ) is dark. One of the most common variants of synaesthesia is the triggering of colors by letters and/or numerals, known as grapheme–color synaesthesia, which is experienced by 1–2% of the population (Simner et al, 2006: 1024). Colors can be triggered by some or all letters and/or numerals, or sometimes only by vowels (Ginsberg, 1923). Colors are tied to orthographical rather than phonological properties, so the words *cat* and *cite* would be the same color, while words such as *site* and *cite* would be different colors (Ward et al, 2005: 28). The sound (ɪ) can induce different colors depending on context (Dixon et al, 2006: 243), while the large numbers of participants (grapheme-color synaesthetes) share significant letter-color preferences showing that the vowel (a) tends to be red (Baron-Cohen et al, 1993: 419) due to the higher frequency graphemes (a) tend to pair with higher frequency color terms (red) (Simner, 2005: 1069). In one of the following chapters we will be dealing with absolute pitch and vowel relation, and there will be discussion about the phenomenon of tone synaesthesia, meaning the ability of some rare musicians to have absolute pitch ability and to see colors of tone pitches (Petrovic et al, 2012a). However, it may be a problem for some of them who also have the grapheme-color synaesthesia (if Sol is seen as red, and the vowel (ɒ) as yellow, for example). Maybe those two types of synaesthesia never coincide due to the differences in music and linguistic perception and mental configuration.

Vowels have a key role in language evolution as they play a decisive role in generating the sound or the sonority of syllables in both singing and speech (Fenk-Oczlon and Fenk, 2005). It is difficult to determine when exactly each vowel appeared in the history of human communication. If we try to locate the time since when the vowels originated, we should follow the letter which is the mark for pronunciation. Probably one of the oldest signs made of stone near altars, is the sign (a) and its alterations, such as Δ or ʌ in the Lepenski vir civilization from 7th and 6th millennia BC (Pesic, 1995: 4). We also know vowels are produced in some emotional states, such as the vowels (ɛ) or (ɑ) during the laughter (Menezes, 2006) which is expressed in various emotional contexts. Laughter is a social behavior that can adopt various emotional connotations (Szameitat et al, 2009), the affirming social "bonding agent" which replaced the positive reinforcing experience of physical touch (Barrett, Dunbar and Lycett, 2002: 346). Someone argues that the origin of laughter can be found in ancestral nonhuman primate displays and that can be traced back to even 10 million years ago (Ross et al, 2009: 1106; Andrew, 1963; Darwin, 1872; Redican, 1975). Others assume that chimpanzee's laughter probably arose from their panting breathing patterns during play (Provine, 2000). Correspondence between a feature of high frequency and the category of small size brings us to the universal phenomena of sound symbolism or phonosemantics.

It is well known that ancient human aspiration was to communicate with and live in close contact with animals. One of the most obvious ways for human musicians to connect with the songs of animals is through simple imitation. These imitative songs were a human attempt to communicate with domestic animals, attract animals for hunting, or to frighten off dangerous animals (Doolittle, 2008). Herding cultures, such as the Tuvans, have a rich variety of imitative communication songs (magical and ritual songs), which can be a pure imitation or musicalization in a sung or played work (Doolittle, 2008). In order to imitate animals, such as birds, horses, camels, snakes, bulls, and wild bears, the Tuvans use throat-singing (*Xöömei*), initially developed as an aestheticized form of imitation of natural sounds (Levin, 1999). The Tuvans say that all their music began from imitating sounds of animals (Levin, 2006: 125). The Tuvan have eight vowels, which may be short or long, showing a backness (palatal) harmony

(Anderson and Harrison 1999; Harrison, 2000). This harmony produces alternations in suffix vowels, which take their cue from the backness of the preceding vowel: every vowel can be a trigger and a target for backness harmony. Many languages with backness harmony belong to the Ural-Altaic family. Backness harmony requires that all vowels in a word belong to either the front or back class. The additional factor of vowel harmony in Tuvans is that consonants remain constant and vowels change to express different, though related, semantic content (Hinton et al, 1994).

Studies show that sound symbolism exists in the Tuvan language, and that there are possible links between sound symbolic elements in Siberian Turkic and the practice of sound mimesis in nomadic life (Hinton, et al. 1994). As there is a cross-linguistic tendency for high front vowels to denote small(er) objects (Hinton et al, 1994: 4), so in the Tuvan language there is a slight tendency for high front vowels to denote higher pitched sounds or sounds generated by smaller objects (a small bell ringing "kiÑgir", a big bell "koÑgur"). High front vowels may denote more rapid sounds (the sound of feet shuffling quickly "dildir", sound of feet shuffling slowly "døldyr").

A related category to sound symbolism is sound mimesis, a term referring to ways speakers imitate and interact with the natural acoustic environment (Levin, 1999). Tuvan speakers have many techniques for imitating and stylizing ambient sounds (sounds of water, wind, wild animal, domestic animal, birds, crash of a tree falling in the forest). Tuvan throat singing or overtone singing (van Tongeren, 2002) is perhaps the most well-known example of sound mimesis. Throat singers can mimic the following sounds: the rhythmic clanging of horse stirrups, the burbling sound of water flowing in a brook (Levin, 1999). Many sounds that are purely mimetic have found their way into the language itself: new verbs may be readily formed from mimetic words. Domestication songs are more speech-like, made up of real phonemes arranged into syllables and sung to a melody. To calm a yak, the Tuvan sing songs by using the repeated syllable "xor", and the song addresses to a sheep uses the repeated syllable "totpa" (Harrison, 2001). Types of this expressive syllable reduplication is common with Tuvans, and it could entail vowel replacement of the first syllable with the vowel (ɑ), unless it is already (ɑ), in which case it gets replaced with (ʊ). Sound symbolic forms often take advantage of mechanisms of reduplication (Harrison, 2001: 202).

Sound symbolism is typically manifested in correlations between phonemes and related denotata (e.g., English words click, clang, clink, clank, clunk, clickety-clack, clamber, cluck, clip-clop, clomp, clash, clamor). There is the assumption that clicks were part of the phoneme set of peoples who represent the ancient way of subsistence as hunter-gatherers in Africa, and their languages are assumed to represent an ancient state, a primitive protolanguage (Traunmüller, 2003). In the Khoisan language in Africa, there are two classes of clicks, abrupt and short or noisy and long (Bettex and Demolin, 1998). The former have very fast rise time and are about 8ms long, whereas the latter have a crescendo-like onset of acoustic energy lasting about 25 ms. This allows a classification of clicks according to the acoustic features of abruptness and burst as bilabial, dental, lateral, palatal and alveolar. All clicks are to be precisely distinguished on the frequency dimension (Traill, 1994). The different types of vowels following clicks are limited to (ɑ), (ɒ) and (ʊ).

Psycholinguistic prominence of word-initial syllables influences patterns of sound symbolism, the images evoked by particular sounds (Berlin, 2006; Hinton, Nichols and Ohala, 1994; Sapir, 1929). The psycholinguistic prominence is an important factor in determining sound symbolism: sound symbolic patterns are cases in which speakers reflect their phonetic behaviors upon the meaning of certain sounds (Kawahara et al, 2005). The frequency of voice pitch of sound symbolism is intercultural, just as there are some innate abilities and properties shared by all languages (Chomsky, 1980). For example, the similarity in accentuation between different languages lies in their common genetic origin.

Chapter 3

Genetic origins of vowels

Linguistic ability manifests itself without being taught, because people are born to learn the sound and structural patterns of a mother tongue during childhood (Salimpoor, 2013). At ten months infants start acquiring vowels of their native language probably because they are more exposed to linguistic than to musical input by that age (Kuhl et al, 1992). Several brain structures, including the left superior temporal sulcus, middle temporal gyrus, angular gyrus, and lateral frontal lobe, showed stronger activation for words than tones (Binder et al, 1996: 1239). Both types of stimuli activated the Heschl gyrus and the superior temporal plane, including the planum temporal which is involved in the auditory processing of words and tones. Secondary auditory regions (BA 22) are activated by hearing and understanding words (Falk, 2000: 197) as well as by listening to scales (Sergent et al, 1992: 106), auditory imagery for sounds (Zatorre et al, 1996: 846) and access to melodic representations (Patel et al, 1997: 229). Areas in the occipitotemporal region of the left hemisphere are specialized for recognizing alphabetic letters in literate individuals (Cohen et al, 2002). What is found is the independence of the computations involved in processing the semantic aspects of language and the harmonic aspects of music in the opera genre (Besson and Schon, 2003: 280). Therefore, when we listen to opera, we process both the lyrics and the tunes in an independent fashion, and language seems to be processed before music. In both language and music, words and notes/chords are expected at specific moments in time: we do expect words or chords with specific meaning and function, but we also expect them to be presented on time (Besson and Schon, 2003: 289).

The aim of one interesting study was to determine if two dimensions of song, the phonological part of lyrics and the melodic part of tunes, are processed in an independent or integrated way (Kolinski et al, 2009). Results showed that consonants are processed more independently from melodic information than vowels are. This difference between consonants and vowels was neither related to the sonority of the phoneme, nor to the acoustical correlates between vowel quality and pitch height. The implication of these results is the different evolutionary origins and linguistic functions of consonants and vowels (Kolinski et al, 2009). A vowel is the accent carrier and though makes a sound, while consonants make the sense, or, the commonly believed assertion says that vowels are the emotion and consonants are the intellect, because they carry meaning. The other study investigated the neuronal representation of vowels and syllables in a homogeneous sample of string players and non-musicians. Since different vowels are principally distinguished by means of frequency information, and musicians are superior in extracting tonal (and thus frequency) information from an acoustic stream, the authors expected to provide evidence for an increased auditory representation of vowels in the experts and in processing vowels. The musicians' perceptual advantage in encoding speech sounds was more likely driven by the generic constitutional properties of a highly trained auditory system, rather than by its specialization for speech representations per se. These results shed light on the origin of the often reported advantage of musicians in processing a variety of speech sounds (Kuhnis et al, 2013). Some findings about genetic and musical ability have emerged: several loci on chromosome 4 implicated in singing and music perception, on chromosome 8q implicated in absolute pitch and music perception. The gene *AVPR1A* on chromosome 12q is implicated in music perception, music memory, and music listening, whereas *SLC6A4* on chromosome 17q has been associated with music memory and choir participation (Ting Tan, 2014).

An interesting finding proves that human genetic and phenotypic diversity declines with distance from Africa and therefore underpins support for the African origin of modern humans and modern human language (Atkinson, 2011). This pattern of decreasing diversity with distance is similar to the well established decrease in genetic diversity with distance from Africa. An ancient population split is reflected both in the present-day similarity between the genetic structure of the descending populations and in the close relationship between the language varieties they speak (Diamond, 1998; Bellwood & Renfrew 2002; Diamond & Bellwood, 2003), which try to explain the present-day world-wide distribution of genetic and linguistic diversities through the expansion of agriculturalists, carrying both their genes and languages in the process. Beside the FOXP2 gene (Gopnik & Crago, 1991, Lai et al, 2001, Fisher et al, 2003), there are many other links between genetic variation and variation in abilities relevant to speech and language. Relationship between genetic and linguistic diversity could be followed between population genetics and language typology (Dediu & Ladd 2007), which proposed a connection between the interpopulation differences in two human genes (ASPM and Microcephalin, which are known to be involved in brain growth) and development and the inter-language distribution of lexical and/or grammatical tone. The discovery of haplogroup of ASPM is approximately five thousand eight hundred years ago and of haplogroup Microcephalin is approximately three thousand seven hundred years ago. This shows a geographic distribution and shows signs of positive natural selection (Mekel–Bobrov et al. 2005, Evans et al. 2005) and because of these haplogroups they are potentially involved in brain size and development. However, new research established that they do not appear to influence normal variation in intelligence (Mekel–Bobrov et al. 2007), brain size (Woods et al. 2006) and social intelligence (Rushton, Vernon & Bons 2007). Some authors claim that populations which have a low frequency of these derived haplogroups tend to speak tone languages (Deidu & Ladd, 2007). This idea is supported by a visual match between the map of tone languages (Haspelmath et al. 2005) and the distribution of ASPM-D and MCPH-D. Y-haplogroup A, the most diverse and oldest Y haplogroup, is today present in various Khoisan groups (people from South Africa) (Knight et al, 2003). Correlations between cultural markers such as languages and genetic markers such as mitochondrial, Y chromosome orautosomal DNA demonstrate that these features can co-migrate and co-evolve over the course of thousands of years for music and genes (Brown, 2014).

Genetic and linguistic diversity are correlated at the level of populations: geographical inter-population differences in allele frequencies tend to match the distribution of language varieties (e.g., dialects, languages or linguistic families) (Cavalli–Sforza et al. 1994, Dediu 2007: 125- 187). An interesting theory about the influence of geography on language brings the idea that northern languages are rough, while southern ones are warm and melodic (Rousseau, 1998). Scientists investigated the influence of geophysics, i.e. the geographical influence on physical and psychological characteristics: the limestone area induces persistence and parsimony, as well as physical features such as slenderness, oblong and elasticity (Cvijic, 2006: 12). Speech of the people from the same social background is alike (Giles et al, 1991): we can recognize the geographic background of the individual according to their speech, i.e. the stressed vowel, its duration, height, opened/closed, roundness and intensity (the research). In forming linguistic attributes (intonation, accentuation and speech rhythm), we are well-disposed toward speech attributes of the majority of population in our environment (also if it is different from our genetic origin). However, each individual shows certain deviation from the pronunciation imposed by the environment, due to the influence of the individual's psychology and genetics. When the ego is strongly expressed, or when a person is under large amounts of stress, he/she starts speaking almost completely independent from environmental influences, in a way that suits the attributes of the genetic ancestors (Bogdanovic et al, 2008).

The genetic hypothesis is based on an apparent correlation between the distribution of certain phonetic features and of blood-groups in Europe (Brosnahan, 1961). It might appear reasonable to associate sound types with purely physiological factors, but the shared grammatical and lexical features would hardly seem possible (Bynon, 1977: 256). According to Hajdu (1975), only the alternation between the front and back vowel is old, whereas the alteration between rounded and unrounded vowels appears to be an innovation which occurred in a number of Finno-Ugrian languages. For example, rounded front vowels, such as (ö) and (ü) form an integral part of the phonemic systems of speakers within a continuous zone which takes in the French, Dutch, German, Icelandic, Norwegian, Danish, Swedish, Finish, Southern Lapp, Hungarian, north-western Italian, Scottish and Albanian language areas (Bynon, 1977: 251). In all members of the Finno-Ugrian language family rounded front vowels are old, and fronting and rounding plays an important part in vowel harmony systems which govern the distribution of vowel types within words (Bynon, 1977: 252). A range of cognitive/perceptual and anatomical/physiological factors could be seen in the case of Italian and Yoruba vowels (Ladefoged, 1984; Disner 1983) where there are small differences in formant values between Yoruba and Italian. Despite very similar seven-vowel systems, these differences in formant values are probably because of the anatomical differences between Africans and Europeans, facial differences and shapes of the lips of Italian speakers as opposed to Yoruba speakers. The second formant is lower for the Italian vowels than for the Yoruba vowel (Ladefoged 1984: 85-86). Facial anatomy is influenced by genetic makeup, and vowel quality might be affected by facial anatomy (Darlington, 1947, 1955; Brosnahan, 1961). This idea is based on the apparent correlation between the distribution of blood groups in Europe and the distribution in European languages of the interdental fricatives, front rounded vowels, and other various phonetic types. It is also underlined that genes have an important impact on the normal individual variation in brain anatomy and physiology, including areas involved in language and speech (Bartley, Jones & Weinberger, 1997; Pennington et al, 2000; Thompson et al, 2001, Wright et al, 2002; Scamvougeras et al, 2003; Giedd, Schmitt & Neale, 2007).

A genetic link also exists between the origin of populations and their linguistic characteristics: each blood type is featured by specific intonations and accentuations which express a unique set of character dispositions, no matter what language people speak (Bogdanovic et al, 2008). Nasal articulation occurs when a part of a phonation goes through the nasal cavity. Such nasal sounds present a feature of the Cro-Magnon type in Europe and of Indians in South America. It is also known that Cro-Magnons live in some Balkan areas, in south-east Serbia and among Albanians in Kosovo (Bogdanovic et al, 2008). The source of nasal speech is of physiological nature, but it can also occur because of genetic variations. There is a possible hypothesis that nasal sounds can be heard from Muslims living nowadays in Belgrade (Serbia) and that speech nasality is the prominent feature for recognizing Muslims. It is said that ghunnah (in a Quran reading) is a nasal sound that is emitted from the nose and that has its own distinct place of articulation (the nasopharynx, without any influence of the tongue) (S. A. al-Hashmi, 2001: 32). There is also a huge influence on a popular love song named *sevdalinka* in 19th century Bosnia and Serbia, not just to the artistic Serbian poetry but also to the type of singing that is proposed for this kind of song (Petrovic and Milankovic, 2013b). It should be sung expressively, with vibrato tones, and glissando nasal singing which present a well-known and recognizable singing style (Milosevic, 1964: 24, 38).

People with A and B blood type speak with dynamic accentuation and their emotions depend on their current reality experience. However, social factors may suppress emotions by raising the sense of guilt. In speech of people with O blood type there is a predisposition for bringing the ego in to all activities and language (Bogdanovic et al, 2008). There is a clear correlation between genetic markers and accentuation and intonation of speech. Genetic marker HLA-DR7 in Europe and Asia is characterized by raising the speech melody and pentatonic scale in music (Bogdanovic et al, 2008). Mutual accentuation and intonation is the feature of speech and music of populations with the mutual marker HLA-B35 (Dalmatia, Alps, Pannonia, Peloponnese, South India, Latin America, Jews). Their speech rhythm is slower, and the Semitic scale and Mediterranean elements can be heard in their music (Bogdanovic et al, 2008). Genetic marker HLA-B18 is the most prominent among people in southern Italy, Sicily, Sardinia, Western Spain, Montenegro and Dalmatia, Northern Albania, Kosovo, in Southern and Eastern Serbia and Southern Romania. Finally, Dinarians live in the Balkans (Montenegro, Hercegovina, Western Serbia and Dalmatia), in Kavkaz, Saudi Arabia and Iraq, in Afghanistan and Pakistan and among American Indians. Dignity is a typical Dinarian characteristic and it is reflected in abrupt rhythm and in the melody of their music. Most languages have five vowels and in the music of nations that use such languages we can hear pentatonic scales (Crothers, 1978): it seems that two or three tones mark a lower, and 12 tones an upper limit (Nettl, 2000). Since vowels play a decisive role in generating a sound or the sonority of syllables (Fenk-Oczlon & Fenk, 2005), parallels between vowel systems and musical scales across cultures have been found.

Chapter 4

Vowel systems and musical scales and intervals

Most contemporary languages have five-vowel systems and in music the pentatonic scale is more widely used than any other. The seven-vowel systems have their parallel in the heptatonic scales, or the six-vowel system in the hexatonic scales. The upper limit of the vowels is around twelve, which coincides with the twelve-interval Western scale (Burns, 1999: 257). It might be promising to look whether languages with a lower number of vowels also tend to have smaller scale sizes. The pentatonic scale in the eastern Asian music presents a widespread pattern, and the majority of eastern Asian languages have five-vowel systems. Arapaho language (spoken on the eastern sea board of the US and Canada) has four vowels and scales of four to six tones, while most of the Aboriginal languages have three vowels, only those from the Northern Territory have five (Butcher & Anderson, 2008), and the use of a higher number of pitches (Lauridsen, 1983).

What a vowel system is in language, so is a scale in music, in a way of its organization as a set of distinct pitches and intervals within the octave (Pattel, 2008: 14). The number of pitches by octave (degrees of the scale) is very similar across musical cultures (from two to seven tones), but the number of phonemes largely differs between languages (from eleven in Polynesian to one hundred and forty-one in the language of the Bushmen, eighteen with forty-four phonemes in English and thirty-six in French) (Pinker, 1994). However, the reason for the relationships between different pitches in a musical scale is much simpler than the relationships between different phonemes in a linguistic sentence, and it may hide in the tempered music system. Cultures with a higher number of vowels also tend to use a higher number of pitches in musical melody (Morley, 2003). However, if we look through ancient history, we may notice that the first alphabets did not contain any vowels. In about 1600 BC, the Phoenician alphabet had twenty-two consonants but no vowels. Similarly, around 1500 BC, the Semitic language system had only consonants. Around 800 BC, the Aramaic alphabet had twenty-two letters, all consonants. The Greeks developed the vowel system of alphabetic writing. After 400 BC the classical Etruscan alphabet took its final shape of twenty letters, sixteen consonants and four vowels. Nowadays, some languages, like the Khoisan language in South Africa, contain one hundred and twenty-eight consonants, but twenty-eight vowels as well (Patel, 2008: 51). Several Nambikwaran languages (the language family in Brazil) have oral, nasal, creaky and nasal creaky vowels, and much more vowels than consonants (Bateman, 1990, Girón Higuita & Wetzels 2007). Symmetry and roundness present phonological universals for each vowel system (Burquest & Payne, 1993: 34-39), but there are some systems which are not as symmetrical (Crothers, 1978). Tripartite vowel systems are the most common, and in almost each language we can find (ɪ), (ɑ) and (ʊ) vowels. Vowels (ɪ), (ʊ) and (ɑ) with vowel height and front/back are present in about eighty percent of the world's languages (Maddieson, 1984). For example, the Arab language has three vowels (Lang & Ohala, 1996). Compared to consonant, there are relatively small numbers of vowels per language, but there are no languages which have only consonants or only vowels (Hyman, 2008).

The universal for the majority of world-wide scales is the tonal center, which is the cognitive reference for pitch perception, and it makes us learn and remember easily complex melodic sequences (Krumhansl, 1990). However, the tonal center is sometimes unpredictable, especially in some traditional folk songs. The famous Serbian philologist and the reformer of the Serbian language of the 19th century Vuk Stefanovic Karadzic, while

Vowel systems and musical scales and intervals

living in Vienna sung a few Serbian folk songs, because notating the folk songs of different European countries was a very popular tendency at that time in Vienna. In the *figure 2*, we can see one of the written melodies in a pure modal - Phrygian sound:

Figure 2. The song "Zaspala devojka drenku na korenku", Phryygian mode.

Vuk Stefanovic Karadzic sung these songs to Mirecky, who studied composition at Hummel, a former Mozart student (Bojic, 1987: 51). Mirecky did the harmonization to those six folk melodies and they are published in the 1815 Serbian folk collection. Unfortunately, given to a composer who was educated in Western musical tradition of tonal music, this kind of modal unison melody reaches a shape of tonal harmonization and loses its natural sound qualities, which can be seen in the *figure 3*:

Figure 3. The song "Zaspala devojka drenku na korenku" harmonized by Mirecky.

Milena Petrovic

The harmonization that Mirecky invented, fits into the ruling Classical style frame, and it is hard to expect that any musician at the beginning of the 19th century could have created a different harmonization. So, instead of the F sharp Phrygian mode, we hear now the D major key. Unfortunately, this type of harmonization entered into Serbian traditional music, and the entire pleiades of future Serbian composers, used the same or similar harmonic patterns throughout the 19th century and during the 20th century as well (Bojic, 1987: 53).

The relation between the vowel and music interval provoked our attention. Many linguists and musicians (composers and theoreticians) investigated the interval size of the spoken word that carries one of the four main accents in the Serbian language (Petrovic, 2014a). The vowel carries both short accents: up-ward and down-ward, and contour tones (in the Serbian language, the vowel carries both long accents: up-ward and downward). Of course, the absolute frequency of tones and the pitch intervals between tones vary between speakers (Patel, 2008: 45). But, it is confirmed that the interval range is variable, but the maximum range is the interval of the octave for the long downward accent (Petrovic, 2013a: 502). In the following example, linguists notated the pronunciation of the long downward accent (in the word *prvi/the first one* and *zlato/gold*) with gradually downward melody which can reach the interval of an octave (linguists Djordjevic and Storm):

Figure 4. *Gradual downward melody reaches the octave range while pronouncing the long downward accent.*

Vowel systems and musical scales and intervals

On the contrary, the short downward accent (in the word *oko/the eye*) has been notated with the repeated tone, or two notes which are a second apart (Peco, 1971: 62):

Figure 5. Repeated tone or two tones which are a second apart as the range for the short downward accent.

The long upward accent is heard as an upward glissando where the last tone can stay on the reached level or to get lower:

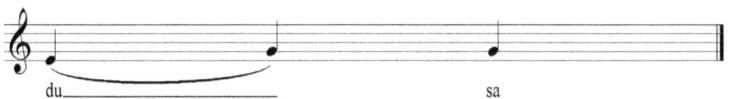

Figure 6. The range of third upward for the long upward accent.

The forth Serbian accent – the short upward (in the words *pero/feather, voda/water, gora/forest, zena/woman*) is notated similar to the short downward accent – the tone can be repeated or there is an interval of the second between two notes:

Figure 7. Repeated tone or two tones which are a second apart as the interval range for the short upward accent.

There are differences in the perception of the smallest units of language (vowels) and music (musical interval). One study investigated the electrophysiological response to matched two-formant vowels and two-note musical intervals, with the goal of examining whether music is processed differently from language in early cortical responses, comparing the mismatch-response to musical intervals and vowels composed of matched frequencies. Results show twelve and twenty-four semitones are perceived as highly as similar intervals (one and two octaves, respectively), while in speech twelve semitone and eleven semitone formant separations are perceived as highly similar (both variants of the vowel in 'cut') (Bergelson et al, 2013). Musical intervals characterized by simple frequency ratios sound more consonant than intervals characterized by complex frequency ratios (Plomp and Levelt, 1965). The most prominent of these theories, first promoted by Helmholtz (1863), states that dissonance is related to the sensation of "beats" (fluctuations below 20 Hz) and "roughness" (fluctuations from 20 to 250 Hz) (Kameoka and Kuriyagawa, 1969; Plomp and Levelt, 1965; Plomp & Steeneken, 1968; Terhardt, 1968, 1974, 1977). Dissonance depends on the ratio of the fundamental tone frequency: dissonance is maximal when the f0 of the complex tones form large-integer ratios and minimal when they form small-integer ratios (Kameoka and Kuriyagawa, 1969; Plomp and Levelt, 1965). Chords composed of complex tones and forming large-integer f0 ratios have fewer harmonics in common and more harmonics lying within the same critical band than chords composed of complex tones forming small integer f0 ratios (Fishman et al, 2001). Musical intervals with large-integer f0 ratios produce more roughness and therefore more dissonance.

Macaques share similarities in basic auditory cortical anatomy and physiology with humans (Galaburda and Pandya, 1983; Galaburda and Sanides, 1980; Steinschneider et al, 1999) and are able to discriminate musical chords on the basis of sensory consonance/dissonance (Izumi, 2000), making them appropriate animal models for investigating neural representation of sensory consonance and dissonance in the central auditory system. Musical intervals with larger consonance differences will be perceived different, while similarity in consonance is used in vowel perception. This perceptual consonance/dissonance difference maps onto brain oscillation patterns in humans and monkeys as well. Musical perceptual space may be organized in nonlinearity and thus music and vowel acoustic spaces are not perceptually organized in the same way. Similarities between vowel/consonance and consonant/dissonance, such as fundamental frequency (higher in vowels and consonance than in consonants and dissonance) and overtones (richer in vowels and consonance than in consonants and dissonance) have been investigated.

We cannot skip the question of the frequency of a vowel and a tone, the so-called physical correlate of pitch. The first and the second formant frequencies are critical in determining vowel perception. Musical intervals are instances of the simplest form of harmony. For example, infants (Demany and Armand, 1984) and monkeys (Wright et al, 2000) show octave equivalence and treat octave tones as similar. The interval of an octave is assumed to be universal – men and women asked to sing the same tune in unison often sing an octave without realizing it, and young infants and monkeys treat octave transpositions of tunes as more similar that other transpositions (Wright et al, 2000). The frequency ratio for octave is 2:1 and it might have a neurophysiological basis (McKinney and Delgutte, 1999): this interval is the most consonant among all other intervals, because of its fundamental frequency and all the harmonics are lined up with the harmonics of the lower (Patel, 2008: 88). The average range of the fundamental frequency variation over the course of an utterance is about one octave, while the average fundamental frequency of women is about one octave above that of adult men (Patel, 2008: 186).

In solfeggio, within the octave, the scale tones are represented by the syllables do, re, mi and so forth, there is no systematic mapping between vocable sounds and the musical sounds they represent (Patel, 2008: 62). Guido d'Árezzo, a music theorist from the first part of the 11th century, achieved relation of the musical interval and the vowel in his famous hymn "Ut queant laxis" (Stevens, 1986), where every scale degree in a given mode is vocalized on a single vowel, and perceived emotion depends on placing vowels on different scale degrees potentially introducing a substantial expressive improvement. The emotional meaning and significance Guido mentioned in the *Micrologus* (containing his teaching method) in chapters fourteen and onward. The unique structure of vowels and consonants within a syllable gives it not only a distinctive timbral color, but also an inherent melodic tendency to rise, fall or stay level. Guido himself writes of how repetition can appear to be elevation or lowering depending on our sense of the accentuation of a word and speed for spoken syllables which are diverse in tempo. Vowels (ɑ), (ɛ), (ɪ), (ɒ), (ʊ) are assigned to an ascending series of pitches when the progression from open to close vowels would suggest a rather descending scale (Vollaerts, 1958) being one of the aspects of the phonosemantics mentioned before.

The methodology Guido employs is to align the mentioned vowel series and that a singer, when he or she sees or hears any group of words, improvises a melody immediately by observing which vowel was present in each syllable. Then a singer sings the pitch (or, more precisely, *one* of the pitches) aligned with that vowel (Green, 2007: 144). In his *Micrologus*, in chapter seventeen, Guido is focused on the specific art of improvisation, and he is continuing the aesthetics of chant as a subject matter (in chapters fifteen and sixteen, see Green, 2007). In the final chapter (twenty) Guido points to the Pythagorean origins of musical knowledge. If we consider that symmetry governs all the work of creation, and geometry pervades the universe by proportions, the construction of the physical and moral world is based on eternal numbers. *Kabbalism seems to have been some core of geometric practice and understanding in kabbalistic tradition had clear links to the principles of Pythagorean geometry (Leet, 1999: 86). They both share the three elements of sacred science: the shape of each letter, its sound and number (Leet, 1999: 11). The union of sound and number of the letter forms the most enduring branch of Hebraic sacred science known as "gematri". This word refers to geometry and implies geometric components to the kabbalistic sacred science most concerned with number (Leet, 1999: 12). In Guido's Hymn there are seven phrases, each begins with the future solmization syllables. The number seven is the most essential of cosmic principles, it is the only one that does not give birth to any number and which is not born out of any of them (Leet, 1999: 138). That's why Pythagoreans gave it the name Athena.* According to Miller (1956) the number 7 manifests itself as a constraint of the span of absolute judgment, the span of immediate memory, and of the span of attention.

Guido educated his students how to sing at sight what they have never sung before and to create new chant – a melody with lyrics. He knew well that a medieval chant should coordinate its musical structure with the prosody, while a medieval musician was expected to be sensitive to words: to the relationships among word order, syntax, and phrasing and to the ways these are related to the connotation of words and their symbolic coloration (Treitler, 2003). Melody functions as a form of punctuation, clarifying the structure of the rhetorical and grammatical design of a text (Green, 2007: 148). A medieval musician might also respond to the sensuality of words: the phonetic level of poetic expression is a sensual phenomenon, i.e. sound. In a good chant, melody honors and heightens the significance of words, so Guido engages the sensual quality of a text, as the ancient concepts of musical expression (the concept of modal ethos) (Harran, 1986: 57). Guido successfully organized the pitch structure of a melody of spoken verse. His melody fundamentally depends on the vowels within any given group of words. There is a possibility that Guido might have had enough awareness of the Hebrew language to realize the mystical sense (which the later Kabbalists clearly asserted) that words do not come alive until we attend to their vowels (Green, 2007: 149). *In Hebrew, vowels are taken as the soul of language (Leet, 1999: 152). The (ɪ) sound indicates the first person singular, the (ɑ) indicates the second person masculine singular (Abba, as the first person), and the (ʊ) sound indicates the first person plural and the third person masculine singular (Leet, 1999: 153).*

Guido might have also known about *gematria*, an ancient system from the kabbalistic tradition in which specific numbers are assigned to letters of the Hebrew alphabet. *Each number has its numerical equivalent of some holy names (Goldman, 1992).* Ten Sephirot of Kabbala (ten emanations) is though correlated with harmonic series: the first overtone or second harmonic is produced with the (ɒ) sound; the third harmonic (the fifth above the octave – Sol1) is also produced with the (ɒ) sound; the fourth harmonic (Do3) with the short (ɑ), followed by (ʊ) and then by (ɒ); the fifth and the sixth harmonic (Mi1 and Sol2) is produced with the sound (ɑ); the seventh harmonic (B flat) is produced by the (e) sound; the eight harmonic (Do4) is produced by the sound (ɪ); the ninth (Re1) and the tenth (Mi2) harmonic with the sound (ɛ) (Leet, 1999: 180). There is a significant correlation between harmonic Sephirot, the bodily centers and soul levels in terms of division of the octave: Do1 which starts with the *mm* (as a central resonance in the head) correlates with the *kingdom*, Do2 (ɒ) with *foundation*, Sol1 (ɒ) with *glory*, Do3 (a) with *eternity*, Mi1 (ɑ) with *beauty*, Sol2 (ɑ) with *justice*, B flat (ɛ) with *mercy*, Do4 (ɪ) with *understanding*, Re1 (ɛ) with *wisdom*, and Mi2 (ɛ) with the *divine crown*. An interesting view that was pointed out is that perfect intervals that are called as such, because they do not have emotional distinction of major and minor, produce an open quality (Leet, 1999: 183). While the second harmonic Do2 is connected with instinctual, mental and emotional centers, the fourth harmonic Do3 may be located in the abdomen. If we go further, each new, higher octave marks the beginning of a new soul level. Harmonic chanting can be heard in the chants of Tibetan monks.

Guido's double melody made of the linguistic euphony can be achieved through a careful placement of inter-echoing of vowel sounds. Guido's melody is organized similarly to that of the words themselves: the music of the chant is based on speech-music, on the sound, not the sense of the words, thus vowels are importantly dominate. The music of the chant is essentially non-referential; it does not express the meaning of the words directly, but the *sound* of that meaning (Stevens, 1986: 301). Guido

Vowel systems and musical scales and intervals

tended to achieve the systematic education of the musical ear, so that one might feel the impact of every possible relation of the musical interval and vowel. The return and the aesthetic impact of a given vowel on the same pitch *feels* different to the returning vowels separated by a mere scale degree. Since every scale degree in a given mode has its own feel as we vocalize on a single vowel, we are aware of the emotion we get as we place that vowel on the scale degree: it will make an expressive difference. The unique structure of vowels and consonants within a syllable gives a distinctive timbre. Guido writes of how repetition can appear to be elevation or lowering, depending on our sense of the accentuation of a word (Green, 2007: 154). In the *figure 8* we may notice the first line from Guido's *Hymn*:

Figure 8. Guido's Hymn "Sancte Johannes".

Guido realized that the simpler a scale could be made, the quicker the student could learn. He also knew that the symmetrical nature of the hexatone made it easier to learn how to sing. He set out to find a hymn which used the notes of the hexachord as the basis for each line and found what he needed in a Latin prayer to Saint John the Baptist "Ut Queant Laxis Resonare Fibris Mira Gestorum Famili Tuoram Solve Polluti Labii Reatum Sancte Ioannes". We may only speculate about the possibility that Guido, consciously or by an impulse unknown to him, knew that symmetry was very important for memory: symmetrical objects have a better mnemonic encoding, recognition and recall (Kayaert and Wagemans,

2009; Stucchi et al, 2010). For the recognition of symmetry (for already known or new stimuli), we engage only short-term memory and don't involve long-term memory (Hogben, Julesz and Ross, 1976). The importance of symmetry as an organizational agent of human visual perception is emphasized in the field of experimental psychology (Baylis and Driver, 1995) during the early 20th century the Gestalt school of psychology, which argues that people perceive objects more in organized groups i.e. formations, rather than as the sum of the individual parts (Koffka, 1935; Kohler, 1929). This organization of the human visual perceptual system is based on certain principles (such as proximity, similarity, symmetry, continuity and common fate). Symmetry perception with adults is automatic, does not demand and is achieved with great accuracy (Evans, Wenderoth and Cheng, 2000, Quinlan, 2002).

The word palindrome comes from Greek, where 'palin' means 'again' and 'dromos' means 'path'. Originated in the School of Alexandria, the palindrome is introduced as a formulation built around a centre of symmetry – a mirroring process which reflects the principle of identity (irreversibility). This could be applied to Guido's hymn and that is, assumingly, another reason for this hymn was of importance, among being useful for memorizing the first solmization syllables. The mirroring form is one of the most examined experimentally and it is considered the most important and easy to recognize for humans (Beck, Pinsk & Kastner, 2005). The preference for mirrored objects appears to be true and for other primates such as monkeys and it is associated with increased activation of the inferior (lower) temporal cortex (Rollenhagen & Olson, 2000).

The interaction between text and image, as we can see in a symmetry proportion of Guido's score, has been established since ancient times. The Chinese use ideograms instead of letters, where graphic symbols represent an idea or concept. In Antic poetry, in the writings of Simmias of Rhodes (flourished circa 300 BC) there are the elements of linking verbal and graphic expressions. In the early medieval times (around 550) songs in the shape of a cross had been invented, while the effort to connect an image to a text we can see in a poem of a Persian artist from the 13th century. The predecessors of visual poetry can be noticed in Serbian medieval literature: the poet Milivoje in 1420, put two vowels (ɒ) in the word *oci/eyes* in the gratitude poem to Teodosija, and in the middle of the vowel (ɒ) the poet put two dots to visually represent eyes (Dufrenne, 1989: 198). This well-known example for integrating visual and semantic aspects is in a Lewis Carroll song in the shape of a mouse tail from *Alice in Wonderland*.

From the score above, we can see the *identity, variation* and *inversion* of patterns. Guido arranged the syllables of this phrase to its motivic structure and composed this short chant in a nearly perfect mirror-form which can be noticed in the *Figure 9*. In segment 1 (Sancte Johannes), only the vowel (ɑ) (and hence the pitch C) is accented; in segment 2 (meritorum tuorum copias nequeo) (ɒ) receives the emphasis on the pitch F; in segment 3 (digne canere), there are three different accents: on D we find vowel (ɛ), on E vowel (ɪ), and on C the vowel (ɑ). The final accented sound agrees with the first: the vowel (ɑ) and the pitch C. Guido was aware of the placement of vowels in the order (ɑ), (ɛ), (ɪ), (ɒ), (ʊ), which had to have some connection with the sound, not just the alphabet:

```
u | a |                                           tu | a | u
o | G |              so                              | G | o
i | F |      ri    ri    lis       li               | F | i
e | E |         ve              ter     be           | E | e
a | D | Ma  a               Ma              ra       | D | a
----+---+-------------------------------------+---+---
u | a |    sup                                   | a | u
o | G | os                                       | G | o
i | F |       pli   in     o     o  ti           | F | i
e | E |       ces              ti       ne       | E | e
a | D |             san    ra                    | D | a
```

Ma - ri - a   ve - ri   so - lis   Ma - ter   li - be - ra   tu - os   sup - pli - ces   in   ces - san - ti   o - ra - ti - o - ne

Figure 9. One phrase from Guido's Hymn in a nearly perfect mirror-form.

Ut queant laxis is the chant which inaugurated the concept of solfeggio, and whose melody Guido almost certainly composed in this form (*figure 10*):

Figure 10. Ut queant laxis, the chant.

Similarly, Jean Charlier de Gerson, in his *Collectorium super Magnificat*, aligns sol, fa, mi, re and ut to the vowels (α), (ɛ), (ɪ), (ɒ), and (ʊ). In the same way Eustacius Leodiensis, John Lloyd, and Romano Micheli created compositions with the strict coordination between vowels and fixed pitches. Soggetto cavato, the term named by the famous theorist Zarlino in 1558, is the similar technique used by the Renaissance composer Josquin des Prez – each vowels of a word is coupled with the appropriate solmization syllable (Green, 2007: 169). The solfegio tones names are ut, re, mi, fa, sol and la. Later, the tone *ti* was added. Some empirical researches found numbers 396, 417, 528, 639, 741 and 852 as the original solfeggio frequencies. All these numbers are divisible by the number 3, and interested enough is the result of the huge database showing that the 168 Hz (also divisible by the number 3) is the habitual speech frequency calculated across the talkers (Peterson & Barney, 1952). The original solfeggio frequencies have been found by the discovery of the pattern of six repeating codes in the "Book of Numbers" (Chapter 7, verses 12 through 83).

When deciphered using the ancient Pythagorean method of reducing the verse numbers to their single digit integers, the codes revealed a series of six electromagnetic sound frequencies. These original sound frequencies were apparently used in the great Guido hymn dedicated to St. John the Baptist that, along with many Gregorian chants, were lost centuries ago according to church officials. The chants and their special tones and frequencies were believed to impart special spiritual blessings when sung in harmony during religious masses (Horowitz & Puleo, 1999).

"Ut queant laxis" is the chant which inaugurated the concept of solfègio, and whose melody Guido almost certainly composed—at least in the form it has come to us. The idea is that separate pitches are being represented by separate vowels, and the syllables lay out the hexachord. When a sixth vowel must be found for the sixth note, the one chosen for repetition (ɑ) is placed a third away from the earlier use of that vowel. The order (ɑ), (ɛ), (ɪ), (ɒ), (ʊ) was taken from the order in the alphabet, but the other reason had to do something with the sound. A figure of vocalic triangle used in education is based on the vowel (a) placed at the apex, and surrounded by the two radiating sides with one being descended from (ɛ) to (ɪ) and the other one from (ɒ) to (ʊ). The methodology Guido employs is striking: to align the vowel series (ɑ), (ɛ), (ɪ), (ɒ), (ʊ) along definite points of the gamut, so upon seeing or hearing any group of words, a singer could improvise a melody to them immediately by observing which vowel was present in each syllable and then singing the pitch aligned with that vowel (Green, 2007: 144). Guido probably thought of the systematic education of the musical ear so that one might feel the impact of every possible relation of musical interval and vowel. The return of a given vowel on the same pitch feels different than its return a third apart. Similarly, the aesthetic impact is different when the returning vowels are separated by a mere scale degree (Green, 2007: 151). Since every scale degree in a given mode has its own feel, for we vocalize on a single vowel, the emotion we get as we place that vowel on the final of some mode is different from the emotion we receive if it is placed on the second modal degree. A syllable that falls in an overall modal design will make a great deal of expressive difference due to a distinctive timbre of vowel and consonant structures.

Guido's Hymn is separated into seven lines, the first six of which start on note which describe an ascending hexachord (the first line begins with the lowest note of the hexachord, and so on). Guido chose to use this hymn as the basis for his teaching system and took the first few letters of each phrase of the prayer and used these as the names for the notes on which that phrase started (Green, 2007: 143-170). Gudio's system is a predecessor of a *tonic-do* system of a movable *do*. Solmization syllable *do* is always linked to the first degree of the scale and for the major tonic. In Serbia, during the 20th century, a well-known method was the one which was based on Guido's. It was the method of Miodrag Vasiljevic, a famous ethnomusicologist and educator. He used Serbian folk songs for setting the basic tone pitches in C major by using the coordination between solfeggio syllables and fixed pitches. These songs have become models for learning solmization syllables with the initial syllable of a word with which a song starts. For example, for learning *re*, the song that is usually in use is *Resavo vodo hladna (Resavo, the cold river)*. This method is applicable only for learning C major relations during musical education in the early years. It is the system that can be used for understanding tone functionality (in the case when following the melody with the basic chords typical for Western musical tradition) and to accommodate to the fixed pitch height. With the new idea of the composer and music educator Vera Milankovic, solmization syllables are attached to words and sentences, so the close link between verse, tonal relations and the sense of spatial tonality has been achieved (Milankovic and Petrovic, 2016: 516). But, the question remains: are there fixed and absolute frequencies for which we are tuning our young students? What is more important is the relative tone pitch which brings full understanding of tonal functions.

However, vowels have a crucial role in determining pitches, their alteration and chromatics. Elly Bašić, a Croatian musician, introduced a change in the treatment of Guido's vowel syllables, in order to reach the diatonic function of a tone. A vowel carries the functional meaning in singing (Curwen, 1858: 346-370, the chapter - Pronunciation): the vowel (I) has the function of the upper leading tone; the vowel (ɛ) is opened and bright, moves freely; the vowel (ɛ) is neutral and has the function to determine a major or a minor key; the vowel (ʊ) has the function of the lower leading tone (Bašić, 1958: IX). In the case of altered tones, Bašić continues, the function is being changed, and it becomes the leading tone, so it receives a new vowel. In this way, the intonation may be a bit better, due to C sharp always being a bit higher than D flat. If we sing a syllable *di* for C-sharp (instead of being *do*), or *rʊ* for D flat (instead of being *re*), we can reach a more precise intonation in singing (Bašić, 1958). Therefore, all sharps receive the ending I, and all flats the ending ʊ (Kazić, 2013: 103). If we know that the vowel (I) is a high front vowel, then we may understand the reason for taking the syllable *di* for C sharp (a tendency for a vowel [I] is to sound higher). The role of a high front vowel (ʊ) is to lower the pitch with its back tongue position. These vowel changes, induced by reasons of function and intonation, recall the similar phenomena in some languages, such as the Kisa language (in Kenya). There are (I), (ɛ), (ɑ), (ɒ), (ʊ) vowels, and their mutual changes indicate the meaning: *rekela*=set trap, *rekula*=spring trap; *fungila*=to lock, *fungula*=unlock. For setting a trap, the Kisa people use the low front vowel (ɛ), but for springing the trap they use a high back vowel (ʊ). In both cases, low front and high back vowels may have the phonosemantic role. In the Austrian dialect of Lena, there is a change of vowels in plural: *tsubu – tsobos* (wolf – wolves) (Rose and Walker, 254). As a result, a high back vowel (ʊ) has been changed in the close mid-back rounded vowel (ɒ) in plural. It might be possible that phonosemantics are related to absolute pitch, due to ideophones representing related classes of meanings through the use of common phonetic forms.

Chapter 5

Vowels and absolute pitch

Absolute pitch is generally defined as the ability to name or produce a note of particular pitch in the absence of a reference note. As being rare in our culture (Bachem, 1955; Profita and Bidder, 1988; Takeuchi and Hulse, 1993), absolute pitch is prevalent among highly accomplished musicians, but it is not necessarily accompanied by superior musical skills. Absolute pitch is sub-served by brain regions that underlie speech processing (Schlaug, 2003; Zatorre et al, 1998). The prevalence of absolute pitch is inversely related to the age and musical training (Bachem, 1955; Miyazaki, 1988; Profita and Bidder, 1988; Sergeant, 1969). In tone languages, words lexical meanings depend on the tones during which they are pronounced: lexical tones are defined both by their pitch heights and their pitch contours.

Although infants use absolute pitch cues when learning about the structure of nonlinguistic tone sequences (Saffran et al, 2005), and the absolute pitch is inevitable for speaking, this category disappears exactly in the speaking phase, almost at the same time when the ability to determine sound of non native language is formed. During sixth month of age, babies learn the particular vowel sounds of their language (Kuhl et al, 1992) and soon lose sensitivity to certain phonetic contrasts that do not occur in their own language, gaining a sensitivity for difficult phonetic contrasts in their native language (Polka et al, 2001), and also for differences in speech, gender and speech rate (Kuhl, 2004). Maybe, the only human ability to produce vowels led humans toward the language localism, instead of the language universality, which is the feature of almost all animal species (Petrovic & Ljubinkovic, 2011). If we go a month further, around the sixth month babies begin to produce nonsense syllables such as (ba) or (da) in repetitive sequences (Locke, 1973). So-called babbling, as the nucleus form of the language, presents the phase of entering into the structure of language. Babbling is spontaneous and not the simple imitation of adult speech, due to deaf babies also producing those syllables even though they have no experience with the speech of others (Oller and Eilers, 1988). Interesting enough, the period when infants start walking concurs with the babbling phase. Parents can understand an infants' pre-lingual speech according to intonation, duration, pitches and intensity of the sound. After babbling, when an infant starts cooing, it recognizes only the vowels of its native language, so the infant becomes strongly connected to the environment. Around twelve and fifteen months, an infant uses one word to determine a few objects, and according to accent, intonation, rhythm and intensity, the surrounding implies what object the infant has named. Similarly, in some languages, such as Chinese or Vietnamese, the meaning of one word depends on its tone pitch. With animals (bats, wolves, birds and apes), a certain tone pitch or sound pattern is always associated with the social context. In Neanderthals (Mithen, 2005) and some animals, the form of absolute pitch has been observed. Namely, the sound pattern of the rooster or a turtledove, for example, is unchangeable and associated to certain social functions – searching for food or a partner (Brown, 1999). An interesting appendix to the theory of absolute pitch origin can be the act that mothers, when singing the same song to infants on different occasions separated by a week or more, use identical pitch level and tempo (Bergeson & Trehub, 2002). It can be explained by the ritualized singing performance of mothers and its repetitions and frequent singing to infants which implicate motor, pitch and mood-dependent memory: if singing to infants affects maternal mood, it could contribute to the stability of pitch and tempo (Eich & Macaulay, 2000).

Similarly, there is a distinct connection between absolute pitch and tone languages (Deutch, 2009) where the meaning depends on the pitch. Those languages could be the proof of a hypothesis that music and language share the same origin (Mithen, 2005) or that absolute pitch originated as a feature of speech (Deutch et al, 2004). In tonal languages, linguistic information depends on pitch height, so they directly correlate to absolute pitch. However, linguistic messages can be transmitted with some musical instruments (the talking drum of West Africa) which mimic the tones or rhythm of a tonal language, or a pitch-based whistled speech (Chinantecan language of Mexico). In the Serbian language, for example, the same word pronounced with a different stressed vowel (short or long) completely changes the meaning of that word (*lȗk/bow[arrow]* or *arc*, *lȕk/the onion*). The same is in the Japanese and Estonian language, where a word changes its meaning according to the vowel duration: in Estonian the word *sata* can mean *hundred*, *send* and *get*, depending on the length of the first vowel (ɑ) (Patel, 2008: 114). It is probably because of the influence that stress has on vowel duration (Dauer, 1987). On one side, there are long/short syllables (rhythmic patterning), and on the other, the relation between syllable and pitch accent (tonal patterning).

It has been found that native speakers of two different tone languages (Mandarin and Vietnamese) display a remarkably precise form of absolute pitch in enunciating words. It is proposed that absolute pitch may have evolved as a feature of speech, analogous to other features such as vowel quality. It is also conjectured that tone language speakers generally acquire this feature during the first year of life, in the critical period when infants acquire other features of their native language. For speakers of non-tonal languages, the acquisition of absolute pitch by rare individuals may be associated with a critical period of unusually long duration, so that it extends to the age at which the child can begin taking music lessons. According to this line of reasoning, the potential for acquiring absolute pitch is universal at birth (Saffran et al, 2005), and can be realized by giving the infant the opportunity to associate pitches with verbal labels during the first year or so of life (Deutsch, 2002). AP is a process of 'phonemic categorization' due to its naming is a relation between pitch-class and pitch-name (Cohen et al, 1990). NAP musicians tend to confuse a 261 Hz tone (Do) more often with Sol than with La. The question is whether one hemisphere is more responsible than the other in the confusion of notes with similar labels. The results indicate that absolute pitch has strong verbal bases, at least from a cognitive point of view, and that in NAP and AP musicians there is a right hemispheric disadvantage in the retrieval of the verbal label to be assigned to the perceived pitch (Brancucci et al, 2009).

Some authors searched for ethnic and genetic origins of absolute pitch (Deutsch et al, 2009). It has been found that AP exists more among music students of Asian origin than among Americans. It is then concluded that AP is related to the tone languages (Mandarin, Vietnamese, etc.). However, it has been reported that AP even higher exists among Japanese music students, despite Japanese is not a tonal language, but a pitch-accent language (Miyazaki & Ogawa, 2006). The reason might be early beginning of systematic keyboard-based music training, where the emphasis is put on use of the '*fixed-doh*' solfège system (Sergeant and Vraka, 2014). The similar discovery has been found in some other studies on AP (Petrovic et al, 2012a). This support the idea of functional differences between AP and pitch factors of speech.

Compared to genetic heritage, cultural experience more influences development of absolute pitch (Deutch, 2007; Trehub, 2008). We can assume that transposition has a great influence on absolute pitch reduction (Watt, 1917; Mito, 2003), and the other possible reason could be the temper system: pitches of 'black' keys on the keyboard were identified less accurately than those of 'white' keys (Boggs, 1907; Gough, 1922, Vraka, 2010; Takeuchi & Hulse, 1993; Miyazaki, 1990; Sergeant, 1969; Zeitlin, 1964). This supported the idea of an environmental influence in AP.

The absolute pitch phenomenon might be linked to vocal production and memorization of vocal tract movements: timbral contrasts of speech are a result of the continuous change in the shape of the vocal tract, consonants are produced by narrowing/closure of the vocal tract, while for vowels production there is an unimpeded flow of air from the lungs (Patel, 2008: 52). On the other hand, music systems are rarely based on the timbral contrast organization, but one example of a timbral contrast is a drone pattern usually consisting of the interval of the fifth in the accompanied voice (existing in some world traditional music and Tibetan monks chanting) that may reflect the overtone phenomenon.

There is a proven link between highly familiar melodies and the ability of absolute pitch (Levitin, 1994) – listeners can recognize the same melody in different registers or keys. We believe that melodic contour plays a significant role in melody recognition – not the interval size, but ups and downs in melodic patterns (Patel, 2008: 23). Interesting research has been made to show deviation of a tone from the center frequency caused by expressive purposes (Sundberg & Himonides, 2013). If it does not constitute an error of intonation, it then shows frequency analysis of performances by singers who systematically sharpened tones during emotionally charged passages (Sundberg & Himonides, 2013; Rapoport, 1996: 112–13).

The physical correlate of pitch is frequency, determined in cycles per second – Hertz. Each octave is divided in the equally tempered twelve tone system, such that each note is approximately six percent higher in frequency than the note below. The twelve semitones of an octave are the so-called tonal material of Western music and the frequency ratios between these semitones dated back from Pythagoras who was the first one that we know who studied the sound of overtones and reported it. Some authors speak about the mystical power of those numbers and their frequency ratios (Walker, 1990), while others thinks about the mental framework for sound perception is in a constant tuning of itself (McQueen et al, 2006). But, there are examples of the ancient Peruvian panpipes and Australian aboriginal singing showing musical pitch relations organized in a linear, rather than a logarithmic basis (Haeberli, 1979). Non-western music systems surely do not use fixed pitch schemes and it is unlikely that their tuning relies on the standardized tuning system of Western music. Our modern day music scale is out of sync from the original solfeggio frequencies and is, consequently, more dissonant as it is based upon the twelve-tone equal temperament. In ancient times, the musical scale was called "Just Intonation". Our modern music falls within the A 440 hz frequency, which was changed from A 417 hz, around 1914.

There is a long discussion on the chamber tone frequency being 440 Hz (Rudhyar, 1922, Sergeant and Vraka, 2014), including the conspiracy theory saying that Nazi via Radio Berlin organized to raise the concert pitch at the London congress in 1939 (Rosenfeld, 1988). The other reason for raising the pitch was that instrument makers wished to export their instruments to the United States, where the influence of jazz had raised the pitch to 440 and well beyond (Rosenfeld, 1988). In 1999, The Schiller Institute circulated a petition for changing concert pitch from A being 440 Hz back to 432 Hz, which they call "Verdi tuning" because Giuseppe Verdi first sought to stop the increase in pitch to which orchestras were tuned, indicating that 432 Hz was slightly more optimal (Rosen, 1995). Verdi himself asked the Music Commission of the Italian Government to change the classical tuning of A 432 Hz in order to respect singing voices: "as music being a universal language, why should and A in Paris be a B flat in Rome?" (Raimondi, 1996). More than a century before Verdi, French acoustic physicist Joseph Sauveur, researched and proposed the pitch standard 432 Hz in 1713, but he was strongly resisted by the musicians he was working with (Haynes, 2002).

According to some researchers, the 432 Hz frequency is in balance with nature and the vocal chords of singers will not be damaged in higher ranges due to the harmonic overtones being whole numbers (the other A's are 27, 54, 108, 216, 864, 1728 and so on) (Haynes, 2002). What is more intriguing is that DNA researchers have proven that the human body lives in harmony and that health has its own harmonic threshold. The number 256 (the frequency for the tone C, if the chamber tone is 432 Hz) is the vital number and the highest absorption threshold of DNA (Feliciangeli, 1996). Encephalographic tests have proven that "living tissues emit and absorb electromagnetic frequencies, and the musical scale has a relation to biological spectra." (Feliciangeli, 1996). Therefore, C=256 is not only the ideal tuning for the voice, but also the first vital step in molecular biology (Celani and Wolfe, 1996).

If absolute pitch is an inborn ability and is genetically confirmed, what is happens if the concert pitch frequency suddenly changes, and what is the frequency that we are born with and tuned to? Pitch perception tends to go sharp as subjects age (for a semi-tone by middle-age and a full-tone sharp as a subject enters the sixties), and absolute pitch possessors tend to err on G sharp more than any other tone – most often G sharp is misidentify as an A tone (Athos et al, 2007). It is probably because the actual frequency of A used in tuning varies widely in history and today (from 415 in early music to 446 in some orchestras). Some authors believe that AP possessors who acquired AP in context of a piano tuned to a pitch A 440 Hz, have problems with producing music that was tuned to a pitch other than the standardized frequency (Sergeant and Vraka, 2014: 221). To conclude, absolute pitch possessors accommodate a wide range of frequencies in their naming of A, which is not the case for the piano tones, since piano is generally tuned to A 440 Hz (Athos et al, 2007) and for the other tones which absolute pitch possessors recognize with no further oscillation. The question remains whether or not absolute pitch matches universal frequency or if a genetic factor is adoptable to the frequent change of the chamber-tone frequency? Pitch memory might be widespread among ordinary people, because repeated exposure to a song creates a memory representation that preserves the actual pitch of the song (Levitin, 1994). The latent absolute pitch memory may be a more widespread trait within the population than the traditional AP labeling ability (Jakubowski and Mullensiefen, 2013). Factors that may contribute to latent AP memory are relative pitch memory and the quality and degree of music-elicited emotions impact on latent AP memory (Jakubowski and Mullensiefen, 2013). The AP is mainly a feature of speech, and if speech and therefore vowels reflect different emotions, then these emotions have an impact on the AP. Consequently, vowels have a significant role in expressing emotions.

Chapter 6

Vowels and emotions

The human voice alters under various emotional states and this alteration can be witnessed in acoustic parameters of loudness, resonance, timbre and pitch (Spencer, 1855). Complaining and suffering are heard through the use of high pitch; contempt and disgust are shown by blowing out often producing the sound *pooh*; astonishment is signaled by a rapid inhalation followed by an *oh* sound, surprise is expressed through a high pitched inhale with the sound of *ah* (or *ow*); fear is heard through the trembling quality of the voice; agony and pain through the use of either deep groans or high piercing screams; enjoyment and amusement as expressed through laughter and the sound of the vowels (ɒ) and (ɑ) (with men) and (ɛ) and (ɪ) (with women and children) (Darwin, 1872). Darwin observed vocal expression of emotion and some vowels linked with certain emotional states: ɒ/ɑ with enjoyment, ɛ/ɪ with amusement, (ɑ) with surprise, (ɒ) with alarm. A joyful facial expression and interest is (sometimes) accompanied by the vocalization of the vowel (ɛ), sadness most often signaled with the vowels (ɪ) and (ɛ), while anger with the open vowel (ɑ) (Burt, 1994: 66). Among main emotional states, only for sadness is the pitch low, pitch range is narrow, pitch variation small, pitch contour is down, loudness soft, tempo is slow, with few harmonics (Scherer & Oshinsky, 1977: 340).

It has been hypothesized that the emotion that we experience when we listen to music has its roots in the expression of emotion through the voice (Spencer, 1855; Darwin, 1872): emotional speech is related to vocal music probably because of the muscular action that the voice is affected by (Meyer, 1956; Merriam, 1964; Radocy & Boyle, 1979; Sundberg, 1982; Konecni, 1982; Stratton and Zalanowski, 1989). Muscle tension in the body plays a part in signaling of emotion: whenever we feel the 'expressivity' of a song we are interpreting the muscular action which produces the sound (Darwin, 1872: 89). This is because the experience and perception of emotion involve distinct central nervous system regions (Ekman, 1992; Izard, 1993). The amygdala is activated for most facial expressions of emotion, but not for recognizing facial expression of sadness (Calder et al, 1996, in Keltner & Ekman, 2000: 238).

Some researchers pose that emotion could be mapped in three dimensions: arousal (activation), valence (pleasure) and control (power) (Schlosberg, 1954: 81). Acoustic parameters which describe emotion in speech are pitch, duration at phoneme or syllable level, inter-word silence duration and voiced/unvoiced duration ratio in utterance level, energy related to the waveform envelope, the first three formant frequencies and spectral moment or balance (Yildirim et al, 2004). These are parameters related to speech prosody, vowel articulation and spectral energy distribution (Douglas-Cowie, 2003: 33). Anger and happiness/joy are characterized by a high mean pitch, wider pitch range, high speech rate, an increase in high frequency energy, and usually an increase in the rate of articulation (Davitz, 1964: 101). Sadness is characterized by a decrease in mean pitch, slightly narrow pitch range, and a slower speaking rate (Murray and Arnott, 1993: 1097). Anger has the highest accuracy of articulation compared to other emotions (Kienast et al, 2000). Vowel segments may have a strong potential of interest in emotion recognition as they convey a lot of prosodic information such as duration and rhythm: vowel units present the emotion recognizer (Ringeval and Chetouani, 2008: 253).

Despite meaning that the association between a word-form and its meaning is arbitrary (de Saussure, 1966), there is a possibility that the form of words expressing emotions is not completely arbitrary, but their sound evokes the emotion conveyed: words expressing an emotion are more similar among these types of words than with words expressing other emotions, due to the sounds of emotions (Nastase et al, 2007). On the one hand, there are the onomatopoeic words which sound like the concept they describe (roar, purr, buzz, boom, bang), and on the other, mellifluous words whose sounds evoke the concept they refer to (hush, mumble etc) and are similar to the concept of sound symbolism or phonosemantics, where every sound carries a certain meaning and evokes certain aspects of a concept whose name contains this sound (Locke, 1690; Leibniz, 1765 [1981]; Jespersen, 1922; Sapir, 1929; Firth, 1957; Genette, 1976; Magnus, 2001).

Emotions are innate, evolved, culturally determined and universal, but there are cultural differences in the control of facial expression (Darwin, 1872; Ekman, 1973). Facial expression was assumed to be like the phonemes of a language: "the units of communication were thought to be attached to specific events and experiences in a specific way as a part of the cultural construction of emotion" (Keltner & Ekman, 2000: 240). Facial expressions of emotion are not related to the experience of emotion, but determined by context-specific social motives (Fridlund, 1992). A core set of human facial expressions, composed of specific movements in the brow, eye/cheek, and mouth regions of the face, are probably innate (Sullivan et al, 2003: 120). Most, if not all, of the facial components of the human expression repertoire can be observed shortly after birth (Camras, Holland, & Patterson, 1993; Izard & Malatesta, 1987; Lewis & Michalson, 1983). In surprise expressions, the mouth gapes in an (ɒ) shape. People mainly focus on the mouth to discern amusement, and on both eyes and mouth to detect embarrassment (Edelman and Hampson, 1981). Joy and disgust can be recognized by looking at the mouth area, sadness and fear by the area around the eyes, while for recognizing surprise and anger is included in both areas – mouth and eyes. The top of the face is the area for discerning anger, the bottom for detecting joy, sadness and disgust, while both areas are needed to identify surprise and joy (Bassili, 1979). Emotions are expressed more intensely on the left half of the face, controlled by the right hemisphere (Campbell, 1978). The left hemisphere is in charge of expressing pleasant emotions (Bruyer, 1980).

Opposite to the well-known attitude that emotions can be tense according to facial expression (Ekman, 1982), human listeners are rather accurate in decoding emotional meanings from vocal cues, which is somewhat better than facial recognition of emotions (Scherer, 1981, 1986). The universal expression exists for happiness, fear, anger, sadness, surprise and disgust (Ekman, 1982). When emotions are aroused, the voice intonation changes together with gestures and facial expressions: physiological effects of emotion reflect on the vocal apparatus (Spencer, 1857: 90).

Human emotions have an animal origin (Vigotski, 1996: 120) and facial expressions of emotions are similar in humans and animals (Darwin, 1872). Human emotions have evolved from animal emotions, and have been shaped by a selection pressure for their survival value (Darwin, 1871; 1872). Harsh and relatively low-frequency sounds are made when birds act hostile, while higher-frequency and pure-tone-like sounds are made when birds are submissive or friendly (Morton, 1977). Evolutionary selection involves body size associated with sounds of many birds and mammals: animals adopt the strategy of appearing as large as possible to scare off opponents (Davies and Halliday, 1978; Hauser, 1993, 1997; Ohala, 1984). Beside using visual signals to exaggerate their body size, animals use acoustic cues such as F0 and quality of voice to achieve the same effect (Morton, 1977). Flattening the ears, the tail, and the hair or feathers (Hauser, 1997; Morton, 1977; Ohala, 1984) are connected to high pitched and tone-like sounds which are also produced by parents as a response of care and protection (Hauser, 1997; Morton, 1977). In humans, lip spreading during a smile shortens the vocal tract, which modifies the vocalization in the direction of resembling the spectral patterns generated from a small body. Likewise, many animals make a facial expression to expresses aggression or disapproval (by protruding the lips), which effectively lengthens the vocal tract, and generates the impression of a larger body size during vocalization by the adjustment of the vocal tract (Ohala, 1984). Many animals lengthen vocal tracts (red deer *Cervus elaphus*: Fitch & Reby, 2001; 60 bird species: Fitch, 1999) for the sake of exaggerating body size (often found only in male animals), which suggests its importance for mating competition (Fitch, 1994; Ohala, 1984). Even in humans and in chimpanzees (Fitch, 1994), males have a lower larynx than females, and the dimorphism occurs during puberty (Goldstein, 1980), when males compete with other males for mates, territory and food (Feinberg et al, 2005). During puberty the action of testosterone is increased and its height is related to changes in F0 and the vocal tract length of males (Dabbs & Mallinger, 1999; Pfefferle & Fischer, 2006; Fitch & Giedd, 1999). A female red deer hears the difference in formant patterns due to changes of vocal tract length and prefers the roaring sound of larger males (Charlton, Reby and McComb, 2007). Human listeners use vocal tract length in order to discover the relative body size of a speaker (Fitch, 1994), and can make judgments about the relative size of speakers by hearing vowels re-synthesized with different vocal tract lengths and the fundamental (Smith et al, 2005). Interesting enough is the information that manipulation of formants and the fundamental affects the attractiveness of the human male voice (Feinberg et al, 2005) and that the lower fundamental makes a human voice sound more dominant to human listeners (Ohala, 1984). Vowels following voiceless consonants (p) or (f) start with a higher pitch than vowels following voiced consonants (b) or (v) due to the vocal fold biomechanics (Lofqvist et al, 1989).

Angry speech is produced with a lengthened vocal tract, a lowered fundamental frequency (F0), and roughened voice, and happy speech is produced with a shortened vocal tract and raised F0. There is an overall tendency for the F0 to be lower, and the falling slope to be steeper in angry than in happy speech, and for formants, especially F2 and F3, are lower in angry than in happy speech (Chuenwattanapranithia et al, 2006). Speech sounds made with a longer vocal tract and lower F0 are heard as angry and are spoken by a larger person, while speech sounds made with a shorter vocal tract and higher F0 are heard as happy and are spoken by a smaller person. The size code is involved in the perception of anger and happiness in human speech: listeners can hear anger from speech sounds produced with a lowered larynx (Xu and Chuenwattanapranithi, 2007). Angry and happy speech has ascending pitch contours, increased average pitch, wide pitch range, raised intensity, increased speech rate and tense voice quality. Both angry and happy speech have a faster speech rate, higher average pitch, wider pitch range and a higher intensity than neutral speech (Murray & Arnott, 1993). These common properties easily separate anger and happiness from low-activation emotions such as sadness and boredom, but not from each other (Xu and Chuenwattanapranithi, 2007).

Laughing and smiling has become increasingly similar in humans because both are related to social cohesion and therefore have similar ultimate (evolutionary) functions (Parr & Waller, 2006). For laughter, as well as for many other emotional reactions, there may exist codes based on biological principles other than body-size projection (Gussenhoven, 2002). Laughter is an old form of social communication and it is closer to animal sounds and bird songs than to human speech (Mithen, 2005: 81). It has been investigated that the smile is audible to humans during speech (Aubergé & Cathiard, 2003), and that listeners can perceive happiness or sadness from speech spoken with a smiling or frowning face (Tartter & Braun, 1994). Laughter-like vocalization in chimps can be heard during play and tickling. In chimps laughter the vowel (a) is missing, which appears to be typical in humans laughter. While laughing, the mouth is open widely and the lips may be rolled inward as the jaw gapes. This expression, also called "play-face" appears to be the human equivalent of a primate expression of the same quality (Preuschoft & van Hoof, 1997). In normally developing infants, the play face appears by five months of age. Laughter syllables are predominantly formed with central vowels, although others can occur, and the first formant of laughter vowels is occasionally characterized by exceptionally high frequencies which may be the result of a wide jaw opening (Szameitat et al, 2009: 12).

The tongue tip, jaw and lip positioning become more advanced when they are emotionally charged: tongue tip and jaw movements are prominent for sad speech, angry speech is characterized by greater ranges of displacement and velocity (opposite is for sad speech), while happy speech is comparable in articulation to neutral speech, but shows the widest range of pitch variation (Lee et al, 2005: 1). The effects of emotions on vowel formants vary for different vowels. It appears that other peripheral vowels are more influenced by an emotional change than the high front peripheral vowel (ɪ). Emotion is better classified in the articulatory domain. There are distinct emotion effects for different phonemes: the high front vowel (ɪ) is less responsive to emotional changes and was found to be less discriminated in both articulatory and acoustic domains than other peripheral vowels such as (ɑ) and (ʊ), probably due to the articulatory configuration associated with a vowel which determines the effect of emotion on that vowel in the acoustic domain (Lee et al, 2005). It is likely that the physical boundary effect in the (ɪ) articulation may leave less room to vary the tongue positioning and/or the lip configuration when compared to other vowels, resulting in less acoustic contrast among emotion types (Lee et al, 2005). Vowels (ɪ) and (ʊ) tend to have higher pitch than vowels (ɑ) or (ɛ), because when the tongue rises to produce a high vowel it causes upward tension on the hyoid bone and an involuntary tensing of the vocal folds (Ladefoged, 1964: 41). The closeness of the tongue tip to the roof of the mouth increases for sad and happy speech. The tongue tip articulation becomes more peripheral (or more upward) when emotionally charged (Lee et al, 2005). The tongue tip exhibits the most advanced and highest position for a sad emotion and this tendency is universal for all the vowels (not only for (ɪ)). The same tendency also holds for jaw forward movement (bottom-left): the jaw opening is the largest for (ɑ) and smallest for (ʊ). For a given vowel, the jaw opening is the largest for angry emotion. The degree of jaw opening increases significantly as subjects become annoyed (or irritated), while the lateral lip distance between the corners of the mouth is shown to be more influenced by emotion than by the vowel identity itself (Lee et al, 2005).

The articulation of vowels systematically influences our feelings which present the links between language and emotions. Probably Guido knew about this when putting vowels on different tone pitches with the goal to induce a certain emotion. The experiments show that the artificial words contained more "ɪ"'s than "ɒ"'s when the test subjects were in a positive mood, when in a negative mood, the test subjects formulated more words with "ɒ"'s (Rummer et al, 2014). The results of their second experiment showed that the subject's zygomaticus major muscle was contracted when they found cartoons amusing. Test subjects task was to articulate an 'i' sound (contraction of the zygomaticus major muscle) or an 'o' sound (contraction of the orbicularis oris muscle) every second while viewing cartoons. The test subjects producing the 'i' sounds found the same cartoons significantly more amusing than those producing the 'ɒ' sounds instead. Consequently, it seems that language users learn that the articulation of 'ɪ' sounds is associated with positive feelings and the opposite applies to the use of 'ɒ' sounds. The tendency for 'ɪ' sounds to occur in positively charged words (such as 'like') and for 'ɒ' sounds to occur in negatively charged words (such as 'alone') in many languages appears to be linked to the corresponding use of facial muscles during the articulation of vowels on the one hand, and the expression of emotion on the other.

Vowel sounds are good emotion indicators, different vowels have different effects, possibly because of articulatory constraints: less constricted low vowels such as (ɑ) show greater effects than do high vowels like (ɪ). To predict a certain emotional class we need the presence of vowels and prosodic features related to its pronunciation (Leinonen et al, 1997: 1853). Negative words are characterized by vocalic beginning and phonemes pronounced with the tongue body in back position (e.g. ɑ, ɑh), such as in angry. Positive words with starting phonemes pronounced with the tongue body in high and the tip not in the coronal position (e.g. ɪ) and, at most, two phonemes pronounced with the tongue in back position in the middle segment (e.g. improve, kind). The vowel (ɪ) appears in the soft, pleasant and cheerful category. Happy words start with phonemes which are not in continuation and the tongue tip is not in an anterior position and the body contains tensed phonemes (e.g. ɑ, ɛ). Words expressing sadness start with non-consonant phonemes pronounced with the tongue body in back position (e.g. ɑw, ɒw, ʊh). It is the effect of several phonemes that gives a word its emotional sound (Nastase et al, 2007).

Speech prosody, as patterns in pitch with amplitude modulation and segmental durations (including pauses), carries emotional information in the acoustic speech signal. Utterance durations become longer when speech is emotionally elaborated: emotional states are characterized by a higher pitch and with wider pitch distribution (Lee et al, 2005). The largest degree of pitch modulation or pitch variability is associated with the happiness emotion – the wide pitch modulation seems to be the major way to simulate speech with the emotion of happiness for the speaker (Lee et al, 2005). The speaker's emotion and acoustic parameters of emotions are related to speech prosody and vowel articulation. Hyperarticulation of vowels is notable when people, especially mothers, address infants in order to facilitate the child's acquisition of language and to satisfy their emotional needs (Mithen, 2005: 74). Hyper-articulated speech, such as angry or sad speech, is characterized by higher pitch and wider range (Yildirim et al, 2004). What is being noticed is a trend where people who are born in one place, but during their life change childhood circumstances, start speaking their original dialect in some specific emotional state, such as anger for instance. It may have some connections with the hypothesis that each syllable is associated with a contraction of muscles associated with exhalation (Abercrombie, 1967). Breathing movements are achieved by movements of the abdominal muscles and muscles of the rib cage: movement of the rib cage during breathing changes as a function by the kind of emotion that is being aroused (positive or negative) (Grossman, 2001: 46). In summary, the breathing movement of human beings is mainly done by the movement of internal and external intercostal muscles and that of the diaphragm. When amygdala detects danger, the diaphragm is unable to move into the expression of an authentic emotion: muscle tension in the diaphragm is a barrier to experience, i.e. it is the protective response to what has hurt or overwhelmed us (Green, 2012: 20).

If we know about the psychological effects of emotion on the vocal apparatus (Spencer, 1857), and that muscles that move the jaw provoke different emotions, i.e. the degree of jaw opening increases as speaker become annoyed or irritated (Erickson et al, 1998; Nordstarnd et al, 2004), we can assume that stressed syllables are made with larger jaw movements (de Jong, 1995), and believe that stress is indirectly indicated by emotions. The form of the oral cavity, mouth and lips specifies a vowels' pitch, which indicates specific emotion (Helmholtz, 1863). Vowel sounds are good indicators of emotions, and relevant to emotional recognition. It is impossible to know which vowel predicts which emotion, and it is not just the presence or absence of vowels that is useful for predicting the emotion, but also prosodic features related to its pronunciation (Leinonen et al, 1997: 1853-1863), because they convey prosodic information such as duration and rhythm. For example, three groups of emotions can be defined from vowel duration: anger, boredom and disgust; happiness and sadness; fear and neutrality (Ringeval and Chetouani, 2008). If we analyze the word forms in words such as *anger, disgust, fear, joy, sadness or surprise* we can predict whether the word expresses one of these basic emotions. The word *angry* has a vocal beginning and the tongue body in back position, positive words such as *improve*, put the tongue body high, while words expressing sadness start with non-consonantal phonemes pronounced with the tongue body in back position. Phonemes have emotional connotations, and the effect of several phonemes gives a word its „emotional" sound. The smallest emotional unit should be the vowel, instead of the word (Vlasenko et al, 2011).

The model of music and singing processing involves the acoustic input and analysis, the musical lexicon, the phonological lexicon to the song lyrics and melody, and the emotional analysis (Peretz & Coltheart, 2003; Welch, 2005). Music is an emotional experience which involves the activation of the endocrine system, the immune system and the nervous system (Welch, 2005). After a sixty minute choir rehearsal of Mozart's Requiem, the researchers found that concentrations of immunoglobin A (proteins in the immune system which function as antibodies - and hydrocortisone, an anti-stress hormone) increased significantly during the rehearsal, concluding singing strengthened the immune system and improved the performer's mood (Gunter et al, 2003). The endorphins, a hormone released by singing, is associated with feelings of pleasure, and the oxytocin is another hormone released during singing, which has been found to alleviate anxiety and stress. Therefore, the pleasure coming from singing together is our evolutionary reward for coming together cooperatively (Loersch and Arbuckle, 2013). In one study, singers were found to have lower levels of cortisol, indicating lower stress (Kreutz et al, 2004).

Music creates emotions in a listener when an expectation is not fulfilled (Meyer, 1956). Emotions and the associated physical changes, cognition, personality, culture and ethics are the most important components of emotions (Cowie, 2005). The voice and the emotional state of a mother singing or speaking are encoded and perceived by the fetus, so in early childhood the identification of rhythmical and melodic contour patterns begins (Welch, 2006). However, children with a richer music environment develop faster as far as singing is concerned (Welch, 2006). Singing activity influences on physical benefits such as respiratory, cardiac, and neurological development (Welch et al, 2010).

The well-known acoustic parameters of emotions are pitch, phoneme or syllable duration, inter-word silence duration, as well as the first three formant frequencies (Kienast et al, 2000). In music we deal with the vocal expression of emotions: tenderness is associated with slow tempo, legato articulation, large timing variations; anger with fast tempo, staccato articulation, accents on unstable notes (Juslin, 2001: 314-15). Therefore, vocal communication can be assumed as an evolutionary origin for musical expression (Juslin, 2001: 321).

While listening to the speech sentence, primarily we understand the meaning and thereby the gender, volume, emotion and dialect of the speaker. Similarly, when listening to musical phrasing we are focused on the melody, and may abstract timbre, volume, emotion, pitch, register etc. The smallest unit in language is a vowel, corresponding to the chord in music (Bergelson, 2013). In other words, we compare two-formant vowels and two-note musical intervals, i.e. formants in speech with overtones in music. Finally, here we are curiously searching for the argument that a vocal harmony does exist, according to the vertical dimension of the first vowel formant in parallel to the overtone series in the well-known interval order. Using psychology, there is a possibility to compare vowel perception in speech to chord perception in music, where many frequencies act as perceptual units (Patel, 2008: 81).

If a tone and a vowel have their own frequency, and if an interval and a syllable have a frequency combined of two tones (sounds), or vowel/consonant frequency, we may speak about similarity in vowel and music interval perception. Only the interval can provoke certain emotion in music, so the relation between intervals and emotions is universal (Blacking, see Mithen, 2005: 91; Oelman & Loeng, 2003). The major third presents happiness and joy, while the minor third expresses sadness and pain; the minor seventh expresses grief and the major seventh yearning (Cooke, 1959). Interestingly enough, recent research has determined that the minor third expresses sadness not only in music, but in speech as well, concluding that music and language share the same acoustic code for the expression of sadness (Curtis, 2010: 335). A low register in music describes sadness and fear, while a high register expresses happiness (Juslin, see Mithen, 2005: 93).

Pitch intervals and chords are musical sound categories, while vowels and consonants are linguistic sound categories. The rules of harmony and counterpoint are often described as the grammar of tonal music. Listeners hear relations between chords in a hierarchical manner (Lerdahl and Krumhansl, 2007): a chord perceived from a new key area increases tension (Steinbeis et al, 2006) while sudden changes in harmony were associated with chills, or harmonic movements through the chordal circle of fifths to the tonic associated with tears (Sloboda, 1991). Three-note chord changes were larger than vowel changes in the right hemisphere of the brain (Tervaniemi, 1999) and musical harmonic processing activates the frontal language area of the lobe (Tilmann et al, 2003). Learned sound categories (music and language) do not overlap in terms of their location in the brain: musical pitch is perceived in the right hemisphere, and linguistic phonemes in the left hemisphere (Zatorre et al, 2002). However, in tonal languages, where pitch acts as a linguistically significant category, there is activation of the left, rather than the right hemisphere (Wong et al, 2004), and vice versa, melodic contour is perceived in the right hemisphere, regardless of whether or not the pitch patterns are linguistic or musical (Patel et al, 1998). Voice selective regions can be found in both hemispheres of the brain (Belin and Zatorre, 2000). In speaking, singing, humming and vowel production, both sides of the brain are activated – a bi-hemispheric network for vocal production exists (Ozdemir, Norton & Schlaug, 2006).

There are studies showing that learned sound categories of music intervals have a bilateral representation in the brain (Boemio et al, 2005). Pitch interval can vary in size due to the melodic context, vowels can also vary in their acoustic structure depending on the phonetic context (Patel, 2008: 77). Melodic contours play a functional role in emotional communication and it seems that universal Gestalt principles govern the auditory perception (Krumhansl, 2000). But, pitch patterns that we expect in melodies are shaped both by experience with music and pitch pattern in speech (Patel, 2008: 197): the preference for small intervals in music arises out of experience with speech, i.e. the close relationship between singing and speaking can be seen in a small-range song which proves its great antiquity, due to small pitch intervals dominating in speech melodies (Patel, 2008: 221). It must have some correlates with the question of genetic predisposition, because in most music traditions of the Balkans there is a habit of singing in so-called rough-sounding intervals (the two tonal harmonics that are close to each other), such as the interval of the second. When singing in parallel seconds a heterophony is created – the typical type of group singing in Serbian ancient tradition. Some might think that reason for "sometimes hearing the interval of seconds instead of the unison" is due to the effort of singers to sing exactly in unison, what is sometimes impossible (Golemovic, 2005). But, others think that biasing from unison is due to the range of male/female singers (Stumpf, 2012).

Nevertheless, we cannot find stable pitch intervals for intonation in any language. Vowel acoustics in individual speech vary due to the vocal tract differences or the tendency to increase the speed of speech (Lindblom, 1990). Around the second month babies show preferences for consonant intervals and detect changes in pitch patterns when the interval of the perfect fifth is disrupted (Schellenberg & Trehub, 1996). The interval of the fifth is the most important interval in Western music, after the interval of the octave. However, the interval of the fifth can be found in non-western musical tradition, such as Indian and Chinese music, and therefore this interval has a special perceptual status due to the nature of the human auditory system, or maybe it presents the basis of auditory perception (Patel, 2008: 16, 88, 93). Because the interval of the fifth is the first harmonic of the interval of the octave, they are close enough in human hearing, so during my personal educational practice, there were students that could easily make a perceptual mistake when differentiating those two intervals. A similar thing happens when recognizing the interval of the fourth, mixing it up with the interval of the fifth during auditory perception because of the harmonics. It seems possible that humans possess the innate bias for consonant intervals of the fourth and fifth due to small whole-number ratios (2:3 and 3:4) (Schellenberg & Trehub, 1996), but recent research shows that chimps prefer to listen to consonant music too (Sugimoto, 2010: 7; Petrovic, 2012b: 179).

To conclude, facial muscles are activated in vowel articulation especially while expressing non-lexical emotional utterances. Muscle tension in the body plays a part in signaling emotions because the experience and perception of emotions involves distinct central nervous system regions. Some vowels are linked with certain emotions. Laughter syllables are predominantly formed with central vowels. The tongue tip, jaw and lip positioning become more advanced when emotionally charged. The tongue tip exhibits the most advanced and highest position for emotion of sadness and this tendency is universal for all vowels. The jaw opening is the largest for the emotion of anger. Hipper-articulated speech (anger or sad speech) is characterized by higher pitch and wider range. The form of the oral cavity, mouth and lips specifies vowel pitch, which indicates certain emotions, while anger, boredom and disgust, happiness and sadness, fear and neutrality can be defined from vowels duration.

Summary

Vowels, as important speech sounds, are stable sound categories in perception. The position of the first two formants is the most important and critical factor in determining vowel perception, while the relationships among the formant frequencies constitute primary dimensions for vowel recognition. The fundamental frequency gives vowels a speech quality, while a clear pitch and a rich harmonic structure make vowels the most musical of speech sounds. Vowels involve harmonics when sounded at different frequencies, and this vowel dimensionality is analogue to tone harmonics, which give off the same sense for the vertical dimensionality in the tonal music system. Similar to tone perception, factors that influence vowel perception are timbre, articulation and duration, and the importance of vowels lies in their sound and meaning. As being instances of the simplest form of harmony, musical intervals and their ratios, i.e. the physical correlate of pitch, are related to frequency.

In case of Guido's hymn, the music of the chant is based on speech-music, on sound, not the sense of words. The music of the chant is essentially non-referential, so it does not express the meaning of the words directly. Guido prudently focuses on an aspect of words which, by their very nature, have heightened vowels because they are sung. The relation between musical scales and vowels does exist. The five-vowel system has been founded in cultures where the pentatonic scale is dominant. As symmetry presents a phonological universal of each vowel system, Guido's choice of the formal symmetry is not accidental. In Guido's hymn, every scale degree in a given mode is vocalized on a single vowel and the perceived emotion depends on the placing of vowels on different scale degrees introduced as an expressive improvement.

It is also possible to compare vowel perception in speech to chord perception in music, where a group of frequencies acts as a perceptual unit. There is a question about universal frequency, when music and linguistic information depend on pitch height, directly correlating to absolute pitch. If in one syllable the meaning belongs to the consonant, then the vowel, as the smallest emotional unit, carries the sound element. Consequently, we may hypothesize that sound belongs to vowels and meaning to consonants.

There are relations between sounds and the image of size, and this size-related sound symbolism may be based on the size of the oral cavity, the size of articulatory organs and body-size. Vowels though have a key role in the evolution of language and play a decisive role in generating the sound in both singing and in speech. Therefore, the genetic and linguistic diversity are correlated at the level of populations. Facial anatomy is influenced by the genetic makeup. Vowel quality might be affected by facial anatomy, while genes have an important impact on brain anatomy and physiology, including the areas involved in language and speech. Consequently, the contribution of the study is reflected in relationship between facial (mouth) expression of emotions and mouth expression during vowel pronunciation, i.e. do vowels represent particular emotions because they are accent carriers? Furthermore, if accented syllables, followed by unaccented syllables, produce music by their duration, intonation, tempo and intensity, do syllables represent a particular semantic meaning because they are made of different interval sizes?

Vowel sounds are good emotional indicators because of articulatory constraints. A speaker's emotional and acoustic parameters of emotions are related to speech prosody and vowel articulation. Therefore, hyper-articulated speech (speech expressing anger or sadness) is characterized by higher pitch and wider range, while the form of the oral cavity, mouth and lips specifies vowel pitch, which indicates certain emotions. Vowels do have phonaesthetic qualities, because of what facial muscles are doing while the vowel is articulated, especially as it relates to emotional utterances.

References

Abercrombie, D. (1967). *Eelements of General Phonetics.* Edinburgh: Edinburgh University Press.

Ainsworth, W. (1972). "Duration as a cue in the recognition of synthetic vowels". In: *Journal of Acoustic Society of America,* 1, 648-651.

Alemseged, Z., Spoor, F., Kimbel, W. H., Bobe, R., Geraads, D., Reed, D., et al. (2006). "A juvenile early hominin skeleton from Dikika, Ethiopia". In: *Nature,* 443, 296–301.

Anderson, G. D. S., and Harrison, K. D. (1999). *Tyvan. Languages of the World Materials 257.* München: LINCOM EUROPA.

Andrew, R. J. (1963). "Evolution of facial expression". In: *Science,* 22, 1034-1041.

Assaneo M. F., Trevisan M. A., Mindlin G. B. (2013). "Discrete Motor coordinates for Vowel Production". In: *PLoS ONE* 8(11): e80373. doi:10.1371/journal.pone.0080373

Athos, A. E., Levinson, B., Kistler, A., Zemansky, J., Bostrom, A., Freimer, N. and Gitschier, J. (2007). "Dichotomy and perceptual distortions in absolute pitch ability". In: *Proceedings of the National Academy of Sciences of the USA,* Vol. 104, No. 37, 14795-14800.

Atkinson, Q. D. (2011). "Phonemic diversity supports a serial founder effect model of language expansion from Africa". In: *Science*, 332, 6027, 346-349.

Aubergé, V. and Cathiard, M. (2003). "Can we hear the prosody of smile?". In: *Journal of Speech Communication – Special issue on speech and emotion*, Vol. 40, Issue 1-2: 87-97.

Baron-Cohen, S., Harrison, J., Goldstein, L. H. and Wyke, M. (1993). "Coloured speech perception: Is synaesthesia what happens when modularity breaks down?" In: *Perception*, 22, 419-426.

Barrett, L., Dunbar, R. and Lycett, J. (2002). *Human evolutionary psychology*. Princeton University Press.

Bartley, A. J., Jones, D. W. and Weinberger, D. R. (1997). "Genetic variability of human brain size and cortical gyral patterns". In: *Brain*, 120 (2), 257-269.

Bassili, J. N. (1979). "Emotion recognition: The role of facial movement and the relative importance of upper and lower areas of the face". In: *Journal of Personality and Social Psychology*, Vol. 37 (11): 2049-2058.

Bašić, E. (1958). *Sedam nota, sto divota*. Zagreb: Udruženje Kompozitora Lake Muzike Hrvatske.

Bateman, J. (1990). "Iau segmental and tonal phonology". In: *Miscellaneous Studies of Indonesian and Other Languages in Indonesia*, 10, 29-42.

Baylis, G. C. and Driver, J. (1995). "Obligatory edge assignment in vision: the role of figure and part segmentation in symmetry detection". In: *Journal of Experimental Psychology: Human Perception and Performance*, 21, 1323-1342.

Beck, D. M., Pinsk, M. A., Kastner, S. (2005). "Symmetry perception in humans and macaques, research focus". In: *Trends in Cognitive Sciences*, 9: 405-406.

Belin, P., Zatorre, R. J., Lafaille, P., Ahad, P. and Pike, B. (2000). "Voice-selective areas in human auditory cortex". In: *Nature* 403: 309-312.

Bellwood, P. and Renfrew, C. (2002). *Examining the Farming/Language Dispersal Hypothesis*. Oxford: McDonald Institute for Archeological Research.

Berg, Jw. van den (1955). "On the role of the laryngeal ventricle in voice production". In: *Folia Phoniatrica*, 7, 57-69.

Bergelson, E., Shvartsman, M., Idsardi, W. J. (2013). "Differences in Mismatch Responses to Vowels and Musical Intervals: MEG Evidence". In: PLOS One, Vol. 8, Issue 10, 1-6.

Bergeson, T. R. and Trehub, S. E. (2002). "Absolute pitch and tempo in mothers' songs to infants". In: *Psychological Science*, 13, 72–75.

Berlin, B. (1994). "Evidence for pervasive synesthetic sound symbolism in ethnozoological nomenclature". In Hinton et al. (Eds.), *Sound symbolism* (pp. 76-93). Cambridge and New York: Cambridge University Press.

Berlin, B. (2006). "The First Congress of Ethnozoological Nomenclature". In: *Journal of the Royal Anthropological Institute*, 12(1), 23-44.

Besson, M. and Schön, D. (2003). "Comparison between music and language". In I. Peretz and R. Zatorre (Eds.), *The Cognitive Neuroscience of Music*, (pp. 269-293). Oxford: Oxford University Press.

Bettex, S. and Demolin, D. (1998). "Etude sur le symbolisme des sons en lese/efe". In: *Actes du colloque ORAGE '98*, Oralité et Gestualité.

Binder, J. R., Frost, J. A., Hammeke, T.A., Rao, S. M., Cox, R. W. (1996). "Function of the left planum temporale in auditory and linguistic processing". In: Brain, 119, 1239–1247.

Blevins, J. (2004). *Evolutionary phonology: The emergence of sound patterns*. Cambridge: Cambridge University Press.

Boemio, A., Fromm, S., Braun, A. and Poeppel, D. (2005). "Hierarchical and asymmetric temporal sensitivity in human auditory cortices". In: *Nature Neuroscience*, 8, 389-395.

Bogdanović, M., Bogdanović, M., Sovilj, M., Jovanović, L. Ć. (2008). *Correlation between genetic origin of population and its linguistic attributes*.

Boggs, L. P. (1907). "Studies in absolute pitch". In: *American Journal of Psychology*, 18, 194-205.

Bojić, V. (1987). *Vukovo nasledje u evropskoj muzici I i II*. Beograd: SANU.

Boku, K., Asada, T., Yoshitomi, Y., Tabuse, M. (2012). "Speech Synthesis of Emotions Using Vowel Features". In: *Studies in Computational Intelligence*, 443, 129-141.

Brancucci, A., Dipinto, R., Mosesso, I. and Tommasi, L. (2009). "Vowel identity between note labels confuses pitch identification in non-absolute pitch possessors". In: *Plos one*, 4(7), 6327.

Brigner, W. (1988). „Perceived duration as a function of pitch". In: *Perceptual and Motor Skills*, 67, 301–302.

Brosnahan, L. F. (1961). *The Sounds of Language*. Cambridge: W. Heffer.

Brown, K. S. (1999). "Striking the Right Note". In: *New Scientist Magazine* (London), 164, No. 2215, 38-41.

Brown, R.W., Black, A. H., Horowitz, A.E. (1955). "Phonetic symbolism in natural languages". In: *Journal of Abnormal and Social Psychology*, 50, 388-393.

Brown, S. (2000). "The 'musilanguage' model of human evolution". In N. L. Wallin, B. Merker and S. Brown (Eds.), *The origins of music* (pp.271-300). Cambridge, MA: The MIT Press.

Brown, S. and Jordania, J. (2013). "Universals in the World's Musics." In: *Psychology of Music* 41: 229–248.

Brown, S. et al. (2014). "Correlations in the Population Structure of Music, Genes and Language." *Proceedings of the Royal Society B: Biological Sciences* 281 (1774). doi:10:1098/rspb.2013.2072.

Brown, S., Savage, P. E., Ko, A. M-S., Stoneking, M., Ko, Y-C., Loo, J-H., Trejaut, J. A. (2014). "Music and population structure: Correlations in the population structure of music, genes and language". In: *Proceedings of the Royal Society B: Biological Sciences*, 281, 20132072.

Bruyer, R. (1980). "Perception of the human face and cerebral hemispheric differences in the normal subject". In: *Annee Psychologique*, 80, 631-653.

Burns, E. M. (1999). "Intervals, scales, and tuning". In D. Deutsch (ed), *The psychology of music* (pp. 215-264). 2nd ed. San Diego: Academic Press.

Burquest, D. A. and Payne, D. L. (1993). *Phonological analysis: A functional approach*. Dallas, TX: Summer Institute of Linguistics.

Burt, J. (1994). *Body, face and voice: nonverbal expression of emotion in infancy*. PhD Thesis (Drexel University).

Butcher, A. and Anderson, V. (2008). "The vowels of Australian Aboriginal English". In: INTERSPEECH, 347-350.

Bybee, J. (2001). *Phonology and language use.* Cambridge: Cambridge University Press.

Bynon, T. (1977). *Historical Linguistics.* Cambridge University Press.

Calder, A. J., Young, A. W., Rowland, D., Perrett, D. I., Hodges, J. R. and Etcoff, N. L. (1996). "Facial emotion recognition after bilateral amygdale damage: Differentially severe impairment of fear". In: *Cognitive Neuropsychology,* 13, 699-745.

Campbell, A. (1978). "Assymetries in interpreting and expressing a posed facial emotion". In: *Cortex,* 14, 327-342.

Camras, L. A., Holland, E. A. and Patterson, M. J. (1993). "Facial expression". In: M. Lewis and J. Haviland-jones (eds). *Handbook of emotions,* 2nd edition (pp. 199-208). New York: Guilford Publications, Inc.

Cavalli–Sforza, L. L., Menozzi, P. and Piazza, A. (1994). *The History and Geography of Human Genes.* Princeton University Press.

Celani, L. and Wolfe, K. (1996). Schiller Institute's 'music manual' released in new Italian edition, Vol. 23, No. 27, 48-50.

Charlton, B. D., Reby, D. and McComb, K. (2007). "Female red deer prefer the roars of larger males". In: *Biology Letters,* 3, 382-385.

Chomsky, N. (1980). *Rules and Representations.* New York: Columbia University Press.

Chuenwattanapranithi, S., Xu, Y, Thipakorn, B. and Maneewongvatana, S. (2006). "The roles of pitch contour in differentiating anger and joy in speech". In: *International journal of signal processing,* 3, 129-134.

Clements, G. N. and Osu, S. (2003). "Ikwere nasal harmony in typological perspective". In Patrick Sauzet and Anne Zribi-Hertz (eds.), *Ty-*

pologie des langues d'Afrique et universaux de la grammaire. Vol. II. Paris: L'Harmattan, 70-95.

Cohen, A. J. and Baird, K. (1990). "Acquisition of absolute pitch: The question of critical periods". In: *Psychomusicology*, 9, 31–37.

Cohn, A. (1993). "Nasalisation in English: phonology or phonetics". In: *Phonology*, 10, 43-82.

Cooke, D. (1959). *The Language of Music*. London: Oxford University Press.

Cowie, R., Douglas-Cowie, E., Taylor, J. G., Ioannou, S., Wallace, M. and Kollias, S. (2005). "An intelligent system for facial emotion recognition". In: *Proceedings ICME*.

Crothers, J. (1978). "Typology and universals of vowel systems". In Greenberg J. et al (eds.), *Universals of human language vol. 2 Phonology*. Stanford: Stanford University Press.

Crystal, D. (1992). *An encyclopedic dictionary of language and languages*. Oxford: Blackwell.

Curry, R. (1937). "The mechanism of pitch change in the voice". In: *Journal of Physiology*, 91, 254- 258.

Curtis, M. E. and Bharucha, J. J. (2010). "The Minor Third Communicates Sadness in Speech, Mirroring Its Use in Music". In: *Emotion*, Vol. 10, No. 3, 335-348.

Curwen, J. (1858). *Stanard Course of Lessons on the Tonic Sol-fa Method of Teaching to Sing*. London.

Cutler, A., Sebastian-Galles, N., Soler-Vilageliu, O., Van Ooijen, B. (2000). „Constraints of vowels and consonants on lexical selection:

Cross-linguistic comparisons". In: *Memory and Cognition*, 28 (5), 746-755.

Cvijić, J. (2006). *Psihičke osobine Južnih Slovena*. Beograd: Srpska književna zadruga.

Cytowic, R. E. (1989). *Synaesthesia: a Union of the Senses*. New York: Springer – Verlag.

Dabbs, J. M. and Mallinger, A. (1999). "High testosterone levels predict low voice pitch among men". In: *Personality and Individual Differences*, 27, 801-804.

Darlington, C. D. (1947). "The genetic component of language". In: *Heredity*, 1, 269- 286.

Darlington, C. D. (1955). "The genetic component of language". In: *Nature*, 175, 178.

Darwin, C. (1871). *The Descent of Man and Selection in Relation to Sex*. London: John Murray.

Darwin, C. (1872). *The Expression of the Emotions in Man and Animals*. London: John Murray.

Dauer, R. M. (1987). "Phonetic and Phonological Components of Language Rhythm". In: *Proceedings of the 11th International Congress of Phonetic Sciences* (August 1-7), Tallinn, Estonia, Vol. 5, 447-450.

Davies, N. B. and Halliday, T. R. (1978). "Deep croaks and fighting asessment in toads". *Nature*, 274, 683-685.

Davitz, J. R. (1964). *The communication of emotional meaning*. New York: McGraw-Hill.

Dediu, D. and Ladd, D. R. (2007). "Linguistic tone is related to the population frequency of the adaptive haplogroups of two brain size genes, ASPM and Microcephalin". In: *Proceedings of the National Academy of Sciences of the USA*, 104, 10944-10949.

Dediu, D. (2007). *Non-spurious correlations between genetic and linguistic diversities in the context of human evolution.* Edinburgh: The University of Edinburgh dissertation.

Demany, L. and Armand, F. (1984). "The perceptual reality of tone chroma in early infancy". In: *Journal of the Acoustical Society of America*, 76(1), 57-66.

Deutsch, D., Dooley, K., Henthorn, T. (2000). "Pitch circularity from tones comprising full harmonic series". In: *Journal of the Acoustical Society of America*, 124, 589-597.

Deutsch, D. (2002). "The puzzle of absolute pitch". In: *Current Directions in Psychological Science*, 11(6), 200–204.

Deutsch, D., Henthorn, T., and Dolson, M. (2004). "Absolute pitch, speech, and tone language: Some experiments and a proposed framework". In: *Music Perception*, 21, 339–356.

Deutsch, D. (2007). "Music Perception". In 'Listening in the world: Behavioral and neurobiological bases of complex-sound perception'. *Frontiers of Bioscience (special issue)*, 2007, 12, 4473-4482.

Deutsch, D. and Dooley, K. (2009). "Absolute pitch among students in an American music conservatory: Association with tone language fluency". In: *Journal of Acoustic Society of America, 125*(4), 2398-2403.

Diamond, J. (1998). *Guns, Germs and Steel: A Short History of Everybody for the Last 13,000 Years.* London: Vintage.

Diamond J. and Bellwood, P. (2003). "Farmers and their languages: The first expansions". In: *Science*, 300, 597-603.

Disner, S. F. (1980). "Evaluation of vowel normalization procedures". In: *Journal of the Acoustical Society of America*, 76, 253-261.

Disner, S. F. (1983). "Vowel quality: The contribution of language particular and language universal factors". In: *UCLA Working Papers in Phonetics*, 58, 1-158.

Dixon, M. J., Smilek, D., Duffy, P. L., Zanna, M. P. and Merikle, P. M. (2006). " The role of meaning in grapheme-colour synaesthesia". In: *Cortex*, 42, 243 - 252.

Doolittle, E. (2008). "Crickets in the concert hall: A history of animals in western music". In: *Trans. Revista Transcultural de Música*, 12.

Douglas-Cowie, E., Cowie, R. and Campbell, N. (2003). Editors, special double issue of Speech Communication on 'Speech and Emotion', Vol. 40 (1-2), 1- 257.

Dufrenne, M. (1989). *The Phenomenology of Aesthetic Experience*. Northwestern University Studies in Phenomenology and Existential Philosophy. Northwestern University Press.

Edelmann, R.J., and Hampson, S.E. (1981). "The recognition of embarrassment". In: *Personality and Social Psychology Bulletin*, 7, 109-116.

Eich, E. and Macaulay, D. (2000). "Are real moods required to reveal mood-congruent and mood-dependent memory?". In: *Psychological Science*, 11, 244-248.

Ekman, P. (1973). "Cross-cultural studies of facial expression". In: P. Ekman (ed) *Darwin and facial expression* (pp.169-229). New York: Academic Press.

Ekman, P. (1982). "Methods of measuring facial action". In: K. R. Scherer and P. Ekman, *Handbook of methods in nonverbal behavior research* (pp.45-90). Cambridge: Cambridge University Press.

Ekman, P. (1992). "An Argument for Basic Emotions". In: *Cognition and Emotion*, 6 (3/4), 169-200.

Erickson, D. (1998). "Effects of Contrastive Emphasis on Jaw Opening". In: *Phonetica*, 55(3), 147-169.

Eschrich, S., Munte, T. F., Altenmuller, E. O. (2008). "Unforgettable film music: the role of emotion in episodic long-term memory for music". In: *BMC Neuroscience*, 9(48).

Evans, C. S., Wenderoth, P., Cheng, K. (2000). "Detection of bilateral symmetry in complex biological images". In: *Perception*, 29(1), 31 – 42.

Evans, P. D., Gilbert, S. L., Mekel–Bobrov, N., Vallender, E. J., Anderson, J. R., Vaez–Azizi, L. M., Tishkoff, S. A., Hudson, R. R. and Lahn, B. T. (2005). "Microcephalin, a gene regulating brain size, continues to evolve adaptively in humans". In: *Science*, 309, 1717-1720.

Falk, D. (2000). *Primate Diversity*. New York: Norton.

Feinberg, D. R., Jones, B. C., Little, A. C., Burt, D. M., Perrett, D. I. (2005). "Manipulations of fundamental and formant frequencies influence the attractiveness of human male voices". In: *Animal Behavior*, 69, 561-568.

Feliciangeli, F. M. (1996). "Tuning and health: an issue of hannony". In: *Executive Intelligence Review*, Vol. 23, No. 33, 28-30.

Fenk-Oczlon, G., & Fenk, A. (1999). Cognition, quantitative linguistics, and systemic typology. *Linguistic Typology*, 3(2), 151-178.

Fenk-Oczlon, G. and Fenk, A. (2005). "Cognitive constraints on the organization of language and music". In B.G. Bara, L. Barsalou and M. Bucciarelli (Eds.), *Proceedings of the Twenty Seventh Annual Conference of the Cognitive Science Society* (p. 2476). Mahwah, NJ: Erlbaum.

Fenk-Oczlon, G. and Fenk, A. (2005). "Cross-linguistic correlations between size of syllables, number of cases, and adposition order". In: *Sprache und Natürlichkeit. Gedankband für Willi Mazerthaler*, G. Fenk-Oczlon & C. Winkler (Ed.), 75-86. Tübingen: Narr.

Ferguson, C. (1963). "Assumptions about nasals: A sample study in phonological universals". In Joseph H. Greenberg (ed.), *Universals of language*, 53-60. Cambridge, MA: MIT Press.

Firth, J. R. (1957). *Papers in Linguistics, 1934-1951*. London: Oxford University Press.

Fisher, S. E., Lai, C. S. L. and Monaco, A. P. (2003). "Deciphering the genetic basis of speech and language disorders". In: *Annual Review of Neuroscience*, 26, 57-80.

Fishman, Y. I., Reser, D. H., Arezzo, J. C., Steinschneider, M. (2001). "Neural correlates of auditory stream segregation in primary auditory cortex of the awake monkey". In: *Hearing Research*, 151 (1-2), 167 – 187.

Fitch, W. T. (1994). *Vocal tract length perception and the evolution of language*. PhD Dissertation (Brown University).

Fitch, W. T. (1997) "Vocal tract length and formant frequency dispersion correlate with body size in rhesus macaques". In: *Journal of the Acoustical Society of America*, 102, 1213-1222.

Fitch, W. T. (1999). "Acoustic exaggeration of size in birds by tracheal elongation: Comparative and theoretical analyses". In: *Journal of Zoology* (London), 248: 31-49.

Fitch W. T. and Giedd, J. (1999). "Morphology and development of the human vocal tract: a study using magnetic resonance imaging". In: *Journal of the Acoustical Society of America*, 106, 1511-1522.

Fitch, W.T. (2000). "The evolution of speech: a comparative review". In: *Trends in Cognitive Sciences*, 4, 258-267.

Fitch, W. T. and Reby, D. (2001). "The Descended Larynx Is Not Uniquely Human". In: *Proceedings of the Royal Society, Biological Sciences*, 268: 1669-1675.

Fitch, W. T. (2002). "The Evolution of Spoken Language: A Comparative Approach". In: *International Conference on Spoken Language Processing* (Ed. by Hansen, J. L.), pp. 1-8. Denver, Colorado: University of Colorado.

Flach, M. (1964). "Über die unterschiedlich Gerösse der Morgagnischen Ventrikel bei Sängern". Folia Phoniatrica, 16, 67-74.

Francis, A. L., Ciocca, V., and Ng, B. K. (2003). "On the non categorical perception of lexical tones". In: *Percept. Psychophys.* 65(7), 1029–1044.

Fridlund, A. J., Kenworthy, K. G. and Jaffey, A. M. (1992). "Audience effects in affective imagery: Replication and extension to dysphoric imagery". In: *Journal of Nonverbal Behavior*, 16, 191-212.

Galaburda, A., Sanides, F. (1980). "Cytoarchitectonic organization of the human auditory cortex". In: *Journal of Comparative Neurology*, 190, 597–610.

Galaburda, A. M. and Pandya, D. N. (1983). "The intrinsic architectonic and connectional organization of the superior temporal region of the rhesus monkey". In: *Journal of Comparative Neurology*, 221, 169-184.

Gandour, J. (1977). „On the interaction between tone and vowel length: Evidence from Thai dialects". In: *Phonetica*, 34, 54–65.

Genette, G. (1976). *Mimologiques: Voyage and Cratylie.* Paris: aux Editions du Seuil.

Giedd, J. N., Schmitt, J. E. and Neale, M. C. (2007). "Structural brain magnetic resonance imaging of pediatric twins". In: *Human Brain Mapping,* 28, 474-481.

Giles, H., Coupland, N. and Coupland, J. (Eds.) (1991). *Contexts of Accommodation: Developments in Applied Sociolinguistics.* New York: Cambridge University Press.

Ginsberg, L. (1923). "A Case of Synaesthesia". In: *American Journal of Psychology,* 34, 582-589.

Girón Higuita, J. M. and Wetzels, W. L. (2007). "Tone in Wansohot (Puinave), Colombia". In W. L. Wetzels (ed), *Language Endangerment and Endangered Languages: Linguistic and Anthropological Studies with Special Emphasis on the Languages and Cultures of the Andean-Amazonian Border Area* (pp. 129-156). Leiden: CNWS.

Goldman, J. (1992). Healing Sounds: The Power of Harmonics. Healing Arts Press.

Goldstein, U. (1980). *An articulatory model for the vocal tracts of growing children.* PhD dissertation (Massachusetts Institute of Technology).

Golemovic, D. (2005). *Etnomuzikološki ogledi.* Drugo izdanje. Beograd: Biblioteka XX vek.

Gopnik, M. and Crago, M. B. (1991). "Familial aggregation of a developmental language disorder". In: *Cognition,* 39, 1-50.

Goto, H. (1971). "Auditory perception by normal Japanese adults of the sounds 'l' and 'r'". In: *Neuropsychologia,* 9(3), 317–323.

Gough, E. (1922). *The Effects of Practice on Judgments of Absolute Pitch*. New York: Columbia University.

Granat, J., Boe, L. J., Badin, P., Pochic, D., Heim, J. L., Peyre, E., Benoit, R. (2007). "Prediction of the ability of reconstituted vocal tracts of fossils to produce speech". *Proceedings of the 16th International Congress of Phonetic Sciences* (pp. 381-384). Saarbrucken, Germany.

Green, E. (2007). "New answer to chapter 17 of Guido's Micrologus". In: IRASM, 38(2), 143-170.

Green, I. (2012). "The Role of the diaphragm in Self-Awareness and Transformation". In: RMIJ, Vol. 5, Issue 2, 5-29.

Greenberg, J. H. (1962). "Is the vowel-consonant dichotomy universal?" In: *Word*, 18, 73-81.

Grossman, P., Wientjes, C.J. (2001). "How breathing adjusts to mental and physical demands". In: Haruki, Y., Homma, I., Umezawa, A., Masaoka, Y. (Eds.), *Respiration and Emotion*. Springer, New York, pp. 43–55.

Gussenhoven, C. (2002). "Intonation and interpretation: Phonetics and Phonology". In: *Proceedings of the 1st International Conference on Speech Prosody*, Aix-en-Provence, France, 47-57.

Haeberli, J. (1979). "Twelve Nasca Panpipes". In: *Ethnomusicology*, 23(1), 57-74.

Hajdu, P. (1975). *Finno-Ugric languages and peoples*. Translated and adapted by G. F. Cushing. London: Andre Deutsch.

Harran, D. (1986). *Word Tone Relations in Musical Thought: From Antiquity to the Seventeenth Century*. Stuttgart: Hänssler-Verlag.

Harris, J. (2006). "The phonology of being understood: further arguments against sonority". In: *Lingua*, 116, 1483-1494.

Harrison, J. E. (2001). *Synaesthesia - the strangest thing*. Oxford: Oxford University Press.

Haspelmath, M., Dryer, M. S., Gil, D. and Comrie, B. (2005). *The World Atlas of Language Structures*. Oxford: Oxford University Press.

Hauser, M. D. (1993). "The evolution of nonhuman primate vocalizations: effects of phylogeny, body weight and social context". In: *American Naturalist*, 142, 528-542.

Hauser, M. D. (1997). "Artifactual kinds and functional design features: what a primate understands without language". In: *Cognition*, 64, 285–308.

Hauser, M. D., Fitch, W. T. (2003). "What are the uniquely human components of the language faculty?" In M. Christiansen and S. Kirby (Eds.), *Language evolution* (pp. 158–181). Oxford: Oxford University Press.

Haynes, B. (2002). *A History of Performing Pitch: The Story of 'A'*. Lanham, Md.: Scarecrow.

Helmholtz, H. von (1863). *Sensations of Tone as a Psychological Basis for the Theory of Music*. London: Longmans, Green and Co.

Henthorn, T. and Deutsch, D. (2007). Ethnicity versus Early Environment: Comment on 'Early childhood music education and predisposition to absolute pitch: Teasing apart genes and environment' by Peter K. Gregersen, Elena Kowalsky, Nina Kohn, and Elizabeth West Marvin (2000). *American Journal of Medical Genetics, Part A*, 143A, 102-103.

Hewitt, G. P., MacLarnon, A., Jones, K. E. (2002). "The Functions of Laryngeal Air Sacs in Primates: A New Hypothesis". In: *Folia Primatologica,* 73, 70–94.

Hinton, L., Nichols, J. and Ohala, J. (Eds.). (1994). *Sound Symbolisms.* Cambridge: University Press.

Hogben, J. H., Julesz, B. and Ross, J. (1976). "Short-term memory in symmetry perception". In: *Vision Research,* 16, 861-866.

Hollien, H. (1960). "Some laryngeal correlates of vocal pitch". In: *Journal of Speech and Hearing Research,* 3, 52–58.

Honingh, A. and Bod, R. (2011). "In search of universal properties of musical scales". In: *Journal of New Music Research,* Vol. 40, No. 1, 81-89.

Horowitz, L. G., Puleo, J., Barber, J. E. (1999). *Healing Codes for the Biological Apocalypse.* Medical Veritas International.

Howie, J. M. (1976). *Acoustical studies of Mandarin vowels and tones.* Cambridge: Cambridge University Press.

Hughes. D. W. (2000). "No nonsense: the logic and power of acoustic-iconic mnemonic systems". In: *British Journal of Ethnomusicology,* 9(2), 93-120.

Hulst, H. van der and Weijer, J. van de. (1995). "Vowel harmony". In John A. Goldsmith (ed.), *The handbook of phonological theory,* 495-534. Cambridge, MA: Blackwell.

Huron, D. (1996). "The melodic arch in Western folksongs". In: *Computing in Musicology,* 10, 3-23.

Hyman, L. M. (2008). "Universals in Phonology". In: *The Linguistic Review,* Vol. 25, Issue 1-2, 83-137.

Izard, C. E. and Malatesta, C. Z. (1987). "Perspectives on emotional development I: Differential emotions theory of early emotional development". In: Osofsky J. D. (ed) *Handbook of infant development*, 2nd ed (pp. 494–554).

Izard, C. E. (1993). "Four systems for emotion activation: Cognitive and non cognitive processes". In: *Psychological Review*, 100, 68–90.

Izumi, A. (2000). "Japanese monkeys perceive sensory consonance of chords". In: *Journal of the Acoustical Society of America*, 108, 3073–3078.

Jakobson, R. and Halle, M. (1956). *Fundmentals of language*. The Hague: Mouton.

Jakobson, R. (1962). *Selected writings*. Volume I: Phonological studies. S-Gravenhage: Mouton & Co.

Jakubowski, K. and Mullensiefen, D. (2013). "The influence of music-elicited emotions and relative pitch memory for familiar melodies". In: *The Quarterly journal of experimental psychology journal*, 66(7), 1259-1267.

Jancke, L. (2008). "Music, memory and emotion". In: *Journal of Biology*, 7(21).

Jeans, J. (1937). *Science and Music*. Cambridge: Cambridge University Press.

Jenkins, J. J. (1987). "A selective history of issues in vowel perception". In: *Journal of Memory and Language*, 26, 542-549.

Jespersen, O. (1864). *Progress in Language*. London: Swan Sonnenschein & Co.

Jespersen, O. (1922). *Language; It's Nature, Development and Origin*. London: George Allen & Unwin Ltd.

Jong, de K. J. (1995). "The supraglottal articulation of prominence in English: Linguistic stress as localized hyperarticulation". In: *Journal of the Acoustical Society of America*, 97, 491-504.

Juslin, P. N. (2001). "Communicating emotion in music performance: A review and a theoretical framework". In: *Music and emotion: Theory and research*, Juslin P. N. & J. A. Sloboda (eds), pp. 309 – 37. Oxford University Press.

Kameoka, A. and Kuriyagawa, M. (1969). "Consonance Theory Part I: Consonance of Dyads". In: *Journal of Acoustical Society of America*, 45, 1451-1459.

Kawahara, S., Matsunaka, Y., Nakayama, A. and Shinohara, K. (2005). "An Experimental Case Study of Sound Symbolism in Japanese". A paper presented at New Directions in Cognitive Linguistics Conference. University of Sussex, UK.

Kayaert, G. and Wagemans, J. (2009). "Delayed shape matching benefits from simplicity and symmetry". In: Vision Research, 49, 708-717.

Kaye, J., Lowenstamm, J. and Vergnaud, J-R. (1985). "The internal structure of phonological elements: A theory of charm and government". In: *Phonology* [Yearbook], 2, 303-328.

Kazić, S. (2013). *Solfeggio: historija i praksa*. Sarajevo: Muzička akademija, Institut za muzikologiju.

Keenan, J. S. and Barrett, G. C. (1962). "Interlaryngeal relationships during pitch and intensity changes". In: *Journal of Speech and Hearing Research*, 5, 173-178.

Keltner, D. and Ekman, P. (2000). "Facial expression of emotion". Chapter 15. In: M. Lewis and J. Haviland-jones (eds). *Handbook of emotions*, 2nd edition (pp. 236-249). New York: Guilford Publications, Inc.

Kienast, M., Sendlmeier, W. F. (2000). *Acoustical analysis of spectral and temporal changes in emotional speech*. Institute of Communication science, Technical University of Berlin, Germany.

Kitzing, P. and Sonesson, B. (1967). "Shape and shift of the laryngeal ventricle during phonation". In: *Acta Oto-Laryngologica* (Stockholm), 63, 479.

Klatt, D. H. (1976). „Segmental duration in English". In: *Journal of the Acoustical Society of America*, 59, 1208-1221.

Knight, A., Underhill, P. A., Mortensen, H. M., Zhivotovsky, L. A., Lin, A. A., Henn, B. M., Louis, D., Ruhlen, M., Mountain, J. L. (2003). "African Y chromosome and mtDNA divergence provides insight into the history of click languages". *Current Biology*, 13, 464–473.

Koffka, K. (1935). *Principles of Gestalt Psychology*. London: Lund Humphries.

Kohler, W. (ed.) (1929). *Gestalt Psychology*. New York: Horace Liveright.

Kolinsky, R., Lidji, P., Peretz, I., Besson, M., Morais, J. (2009). "Processing interactions between phonology and melody: vowels sing but consonants speak". In: *Cognition*, 112, 1–20.

Konecni, V. J. (1982). "Social interaction and musical preference". In D. Deutsch (Ed.), *The psychology of music* (pp. 497–516). New York: Academic Press.

Kreutz, G., Bongard, S., Rohrmann, S., Hodapp, V., Grebe, D. (2004). Effects of choir singing or listening on secretory immunoglobulin A, cortisol and emotional state. *Journal of Behavioral Medicine*, 27(6), 623-635.

Kronman, U., Sundberg, J. (1987). "Is the musical ritard an allusion to physical motion?" In A. Gabrielsson (ed.), *Action and Perception in Rhythm and Music* (pp.57-68), Royal Swedisch Academy of Music, No. 55.

Krumhansl, C. L. (1990). "Tonal hierarchies and rare intervals in music cognition". In: *Music Perception*, 7, 309-324.

Krumhansl, C. L. (2000). "Rhythm and Pitch in Music Cognition". In: *Psychological Bulletin*, Vol. 126, No. 1, 59-179.

Kuhl, P. K. (1992). "Psychoacoustics and speech perception: internal standards, perceptual anchors, and prototypes". In L. A. Werner and E. W. Rubel (Eds.), *Developmental psychoacoustics* (pp. 293–332). Washington, DC: American Psychological Association.

Kuhl, P. K., Williams, K. A., Lacerda, F., Stevens, K. N. and Lindblom, B. (1992). "Linguistic experience alters phonetic perception in infants by 6 months of age". In: *Science*, 255, 606–608.

Kuhl, P. K. (2004). "Early language acquisition: Cracking the speech code". In: *Nature Reviews Neuroscience*, 5, 831–843.

Kuhnis, J., Elmer, S., Meyer, M., Jancke, L. (2013). "The encoding of vowels and temporal speech cues in the auditory cortex of professional musicians: an EEG study". In: *Neuropsychologia*, 51, 1608–1618.

Ladefoged P., Broadbent D. E. (1957). "Information conveyed by vowels". In: The Journal of the Acoustical Society of America, 29(1), 98-104.

Ladefoged, P. (1964). *A Phonetic Study of West African Languages - An auditory-instrumental survey*. Cambridge: Cambridge University Press.

Ladefoged, P. and Maddieson, I. (1996). *The sounds of the world's languages.* Oxford: Blackwell.

Lee, S., Yildirim, S., Kazemzadeh, A., and Narayanan, S. S. (2005). "An articulatory study of emotional speech production". In: *Proceedings of Interspeech*, pp. 497–500.

Lieberman, P. (1984). *The biology and evolution of language.* Cambridge, MA: Harvard University Press.

Lieberman, P. & Blumstein, S. E. (1988). *Speech physiology, speech perception, and acoustic phonetics.* Cambridge University Press.

Leibniz, G. W. (1981). *New Essays on Human Understanding.* Cambridge: Cambridge University Press.

Leinonen, L., Hiltunen, T., Linnankoski, I. and Laakso, M-L. (1997). "Expression of emotional-motivational connotations with a one-word utterance". In: *Journal of the Acoustical Society of America*, 102, 1853-1863.

Lehiste, I. (1970). *Suprasegmentals.* Cambridge, MA: MIT Press.

Lehiste, Ilse. 1977. "Isochrony reconsidered". In: *Journal of Phonetics*, 5(3), 253–263.

Lerdahl, F. and Krumhansl, C. L. (2007). "Modeling tonal tension". In: *Music Perception*, 24, 329 – 366.

Lewis, M. and L. Michalson (1983). *Children's emotions and moods: Developmental theory and measurement.* New York: Plenum.

Lindblom, B. (1990). "Explaining phonetic variation: A sketch of the H&H theory". In: Hardcastle, W. and Marchal, A. (eds), *Speech Production and Speech Modeling* (pp. 403-439), Kluwer, Dordrecht.

Locke, J. (1690). *An Essay concerning Human Understanding.* Edited by Peter Nidditch. Oxford: Clarendon Press.

Lofqvist, A., Baer, T., McGarr, N. S. and Story, R. S. (1989). "The Cricothyroid Muscle in Voicing Control". In: *Journal of the Acoustical Society of America*, 85, 1314-1321.

Levitin, D. J. (1994). "Absolute memory for musical pitch: Evidence from the production of learned memories". In: *Perception and Psychophysics*, 56, 414-423.

Locke, S. and Kellar, L. (1973). "Categorical perception in a nonlinguistic mode". In: *Cortex*, Vol. 9, 355-369.

Lang, C. E. and Ohala, J. J. (1996). "Temporal Cues for Vowels and Universals of Vowel Inventories". In: *Proceedings of ICSLP 96,* Philadelphia, Vol. IV, 434-437.

Lauridsen, A. (1983). *Musical scales in Australian aboriginal songs: Structure and social implications.* Doctoral dissertation, University of Maryland.

Leet, L. (1999). The Secret Doctrine of the Kabbalah: Recovering the Key to Hebraic Sacred Science. Rochester: Inner Traditions.

Lindblom, B (1963). "Spectrographic study of vowel reduction". In: *Journal of the Acoustical Society of America*, 35, 1773-1781.

Lindblom, B., and Studdert-Kennedy, M. (1967). "On the role of formant transitions in vowel recognition". In: *Journal of the Acoustical Society of America,* 42(4), 830–843.

Lindblom, B. (1990). "Explaining phonetic variation: A sketch of the H&H theory". In: Hardcastle, W. and Marchal, A. (Eds.), *Speech Production and Speech Modeling* (pp. 403-439). Dordrecht: Kluwer Academic Publishers.

Ladefoged, P. (1984). "'Out of chaos comes order': Physical, biological, and structural patterns in phonetics". In: *Proceedings of the Tenth International Congress of Phonetic Sciences*, 83-95.

Lai, C. S., Fisher, S. E., Hurst, J. A., Vargha-Khadem, F. and Monaco, A. P. (2001). "A forkhead-domain gene is mutated in a severe speech and language disorder". In: *Nature*, 413, 519 – 523.

Levin, T. (1999). "Tuva, Among The Spirits: Sound, Music And Nature In Sakha And Tuva." CD liner notes. Washington, DC: Smithsonian folkways recordings.

Levin, T. (2006). *Where Rivers and Mountains Sing*. Indiana University Press.

Levitin, D. J. (1994). "Absolute memory for musical pitch: Evidence from the production of learned melodies". In: *Perception & Psychophysics*, 56(4), 414–423.

Lindauer, M. (1990). "The effects of the physiognomic stimuli takete and maluma on the meanings of neutral stimuli". In: *Bulletin of the Psychonomic Society*, 28, 151–154.

Lloyd, R. J. (1890). "Speech sounds: Their nature and causation". In: *Phonetische Studien*, 3, 251-278.

Loersch, C., Arbuckle, N. L. (2013). Unraveling the mystery of music: Music as an evolved group process. *Journal of Personality and Social Psychology*, 105(5), 777-798.

Maddieson, I. (1984). *Patterns of Sounds*. Cambridge University Press.

Magnus, M. H. (2001). *What's in a Word: Studies in Phonosemantics*. PhD dissertation (Truman State University Press).

Marks, L. E. (1978). *The Unity of the Senses*. New York and London: Academic Press.

Marks, L. E. (1996). "On perceptual metaphors". In: *Metaphor and Symbol*, 11, 39-66.

Maurer, D., Pathman, T. and Mondloch, C. J. (2006). "The shape of boubas: sound-shape correspondences in toddlers and adults". In: *Developmental Science*, 9(3), 316 - 322.

McKinney, M. F., Delgutte, B. (1999). "A possible neurophysiological basis of the octave enlargement effect". In: *Journal of Acoustical Society of America*, 106, 2619-2692.

Mekel–Bobrov, N., Gilbert, S. L., Evans, P. D., Vallender, E. J., Anderson, J. R., Hudson, R. R., Tishkoff, S. A. and Lahn, B. T. (2005). "Ongoing adaptive evolution of ASPM, a brain size determinant in Homo sapiens". In: *Science*, 309, 1720-1722.

Mekel–Bobrov, N., Posthuma, D., Gilbert, S. L. et al (2007). "The ongoing adaptive evolution of ASPM and Microcephalin is not explained by increased intelligence". In: *Human Molecular Genetics*, 16, 600-608.

Menezes, C., Maekawa, K., Kawahara, H. (2006). "Perception of voice quality in paralinguistic information types". In: *Proceedings of the 20th General meeting Phonetic Society of Japan, Special Issue of the 80th Anniversary*. Tokyo, Japan, 153-158.

Merriam, A. P. (1964). *The Anhtropology of Music*. University of Texas Press.

Meyer, E. A. (1896). "Zur Tonbewegung des Vokals im gesprochenen und gesungenen Einzelwort". In: *Phonetische Studien*, 10, 1-21.

Meyer, J. (2007). "What does the typology of whistled forms of language teach us about prosody? In: *Book of Abstracts* (p. 173), 7th International Conference of the Association for Linguistic Typology, Paris, September 25-28.

Meyer, L. B. (1956). *Emotion and Meaning in Music.* Chicago: Chicago University Press.

Milankovic, V., Petrovic, M. and Petrovic, J. (2003). "Tone constellation: a personal spatial scale presentation". In R. Kopiez, A. C. Lehmann, I. Wolther and C. Wolf (Eds.), *Proceedings of the 5th Triennial ES-COM Conference* (pp. 413-415), Hanover University of Music and Drama, Germany.

Milankovic, V., Petrovic, M. (2016). "Vokali u solmizacionom slogu kao osnova tonalnog konteksta solmizacije". U: S. Marinkovic, S. Dodik i D. Panic Kasanski (urednici), *Tradicija kao inspiracija,* Tematski zbornik sa naucnog skupa 2015. godine Vlado S. Milosevic etnomuzikolog, kompozitor i pedagog (505-517). Banja Luka: Akademija umjetnosti, Akademija nauka i umjetnosti RS, Muzikolosko drustvo RS.

Milivojević, M., Milivojević, Z. (2010). "Dissonant f# interval of the speech signal as a hypoxia indicator". Information Technology Žabljak, Montenegro.

Miller, George A. (1956). "The Magical Number Seven, Plus or Minus Two: Some Limits on Our Capacity for Processing Information". In: *Psychological Review*, 63, 81-97.

Miller, J. D. (1989). "Auditory-perceptual interpretation of the vowel". In: Journal of the Acoustical Society of America, 85, 2114-2134.

Milosevic, V. (1964). *Sevdalinka.* Banja Luka: Muzej bosanske krajine.

Mithen, S. (2005). *The Singing Nenanderthals: the Origins of Music, Language, Mind and Body.* London: Weidenfeld & Nicolson.

Mito, H. (2003). "Performance at a transposed keyboard by possessor and non-possessor of absolute pitch". In: *Bulletin of the Council for Research in Music Education,* 157, 18–23.

Miyazaki, K. (1990). "The speed of musical pitch identification by absolute-pitch possessors". In: *Music Perception,* 8, 177–188.

Miyazaki, K. and Ogawa, Y. (2006). "Learning absolute pitch by children: a cross-sectional study". In: *Music Perception,* 24, 63–78.

Morley, I. (2003). *The evolutionary origins and archeology of music.* Doctoral dissertation. University of Cambridge.

Morton, E. S. (1977). "On the occurrence and significance motivation-structural rules in some bird and mammal sounds". In: *American Naturalist,* 111, 855-869.

Morton, E. (1994). "Sound symbolism and its role in non-human vertebrate communication". In: L. Hinton, J. Nichols and J. J. Ohala (Eds.), *Sound symbolism* (pp.348-365). Cambridge: Cambridge University Press.

Morton, E. W. (1977). "On the occurrence and significance of motivation-structural rules in some bird and mammal sounds". In: *American Naturalist,* 111, 855-869.

Murray, I. R. and Arnott, J. L. (1993). "Toward the simulation of emotion in synthetic speech: A review of the literature on human vocal emotion". In: *Journal of the Acoustical Society of America,* 93, 1097-1108.

Nastase, V., Sokolova, M., Sayyad Shirabad J. (2007). "Do happy words sound happy? A study of the relation between form and meaning for English words expressing emotions". In: *Proceedings of the Recent Advances in Natural Language Processing,* 406–410.

Nazzi, T., Bertoncini, J., Mehler, J. (1998). "Language Discrimination by Newborns: Toward an Understanding of the Role of Rhythm". In: *Journal of Experimental Psychology*, Vol. 24, No. 3, 756-766.

Nearey, T., Assmann, P. (1986). "Modeling the role of inherent spectral change in vowel identification". In: *Journal of the Acoustical Society of America*, 80, 1297-1308.

Nearey, T. M. (1989). "Static, dynamic, and relational properties in vowel perception". In: *Journal of the Acoustical Society of America*, 85(5), 2088-2113.

Nettl, B. (1954). "Text-music relationships in Arapaho songs". In: *Southwestern Journal of Anthropology*, 10, 192-99.

Nettl, B. (1956). "Music in primitive culture", Chapter 4: Scale and Melody (pp. 45-60). Cambridge: Harvard University Press.

Nettl, B. (2000). "An ethnomusicologist contemplates universals in musical sound and musical culture". In N.L. Wallin, B. Merker and S. Brown (Eds.), *The origins of music* (pp.463 - 72). Cambridge, MA: The MIT Press.

Newman, S. (1933). "Further Experiments in Phonetic Symbolism". In: *American Journal of Psychology*, 45, 53-75.

Nordstrand, M., Svanfeldt, G., Granstrom, B., House, D. (2004). "Measurements of articulatory variation in expressive speech for a set of Swedish vowels". In: *Speech Communication*, 44, 187-196.

Nuckolls, J. B. (1999). "The case for sound symbolism". In: *Annual Review of Anthropology*, 28, 225-252.

Oelman, H. and Loeng, B. (2003). "A validation of the emotional meaning of single intervals according to classical Indian music theory". In:

Proceedings of the 5th Triennial ESCOM Conference, (pp. 393-396), Hanover: Hanover University of Music and Drama.

Ohala, J. J. (1984). "An ethological perspective on common cross-language utilization of F0 of voice". In: *Phonetica*, 41, 1-16.

Ohala, J. (1994). "The frequency code underlies the sound-symbolic use of voice pitch". In: L. Hinton, J. Nichols and J. J. Ohala (Eds.), *Sound symbolism* (pp.325-347). Cambridge: Cambridge University Press.

Oller, D. K. and Eilers, R. E. (1988). "The role of audition in infant babbling". In: *Child Development*, 59(2), 441-449.

Ozdemir, E., Norton, A., Schlaug, G. (2006). "Shared and distinct neural correlates of singing and speaking". In: *Neuroimage*, 33, 628–635.

Paget, R. (1930). *Human Speech: Some Observations, Experiments, and A Cross-linguistic Study of Sound Symbolism Conclusions as to the Nature, Origin, Purpose, and Possible Improvement of Human Speech*. London: Routledge.

Parr, L. A. and Waller, B. M. (2006). "Understanding chimpanzee facial expression: insights into the evolution of communication". In: *Social Cognitive and Affective Neuroscience,* 1, 221-228.

Patel, A. D. and Peretz, I. (1997). "Is music autonomous from language? A neuropsychological appraisal". In: I. Deliege and J. Sloboda (Eds.), *Perception and Cognition of Music* (pp. 191-215). London: Erlbaum Psychology Press.

Patel, A.D., Peretz, I., Tramo, M. and Labrecque, R. (1998). "Processing prosodic and musical patterns: a neuropsychological investigation". In: *Brain and Language*, 61, 123-144.

Patel, A. D. (2008). *Music, Language, and the Brain*. New York: Oxford Univ. Press.

Peco, A. (1971). *Osnovi akcentologije srpskohrvatskog jezika*. Beograd: Naučna knjiga.

Pennington, B. F., Filipek, P. A., Lefly, D. et al (2000). "A twin MRI study of size variations in human brain". In: *Journal of Cognitive Neurosciece*, 12, 223-232.

Peretz, I. and M. Coltheart (2003). "Modularity of music processing". In: *Nature Neuroscience*, 6, 688-691.

Pesic, R. (1995). *Vinčansko pismo*. Beograd: Pešić i sinovi.

Peterson G. E. & Barney H. L. (1952): "Control methods used in a study of the vowels". In: *Journal of the Acoustical Society of America*, 24(2), 175–184.

Petrovic, M. and Ljubinkovic, N. (2011). "Imitation of animal sound patterns in Serbian folk music". In: *Journal of Interdisciplinary Music Studies*, Vol. 5, Issue 2, 101-118.

Petrovic, M., Antovic, M., Milankovic, V. and Acic. G. (2012a). "Interplay of Tone and Color: Absolute Pitch and Synesthesia". In: *Proceedings of the 12th International Conference on Music Perception and Cognition and the 8th Triennial Conference of the European Society for the Cognitive Sciences of music* (July 23-28), Thessaloniki, Greece, 799-806.

Petrovic, M. (2012b). "Dejstvo muzike na izrazavanje emocija kod ljudi i majmuna (pan troglodytes)". U: M. Petrovic (urednik), *Igraj, igraj, igraj!* Tematski zbornik XIV Pedagoskog foruma scenskih umetnosti (165-183). Beograd: Fakultet muzicke umetnosti.

Petrovic, M. (2013a). "Music and Language Performance: Music Characteristics of Serbian Accents". In: A. Williamon and W. Goebl (eds), Proceedings of the International Symposium on Performance Science (pp. 499-504), Brussels Association Europeanne des Conservatoires.

Petrovic, M., Milankovic, V. (2013b). "Sinestetske metafore sevdalinke: muzikalnost poetske slike". U: S. Marinkovic i S. Dodik (urednici), *Tradicija kao inspiracija*, Tematski zbornik sa naucnog skupa 2012. godine Vlado S. Milosevic etnomuzikolog, kompozitor i pedagog (68-82). Banja Luka: Akademija umjetnosti, Akademija nauka i umjetnosti RS, Muzikolosko drustvo RS.

Petrovic, M. (2014a). *Uloga akcenta u srpskoj solo pesmi*. Beograd: Službeni glasnik.

Petrovic M. (2014b). "Poreklo muzike – muzika i jezik kroz evoluciju ljudske vrste". U: S. Pajic i V. Kanacki (urednici), *Srpski jezik, knjizevnost, umetnost*, Zbornik radova sa VIII medjunarodnog naucnog skupa odrzanog na Filolosko-umetnickom fakultetu u Kragujevcu (25-26. X 2013), knjiga III, Pagansko i hriscansko u likovnoj umetnosti i satira u muzici. Kragujevac: FILUM, 277-287.

Petrovic, M. (2014c). "Univerzalnost usmene tradicije – zvucni obrasci zivotinja kao muzicki motive u srpskoj narodnoj pesmi". U: B. Suvajdzic i B. Zlatkovic (urednici), *Promisljanje tradicije – folklorna i literarna istrazivanja*. Zbornik radova posvecen Mirjani Drndarski i Nenadu Ljubinkovicu (435-449). Beograd: Institut za knjizevnost i umetnost.

Petrovic, M. (2015). "Non-isochronous meter in poetry and music". In: Jane Ginsborg, Alexandra Lamont and Stephanie Bramley (eds), Proceedings of the Ninth Triennial Conference of the European Society for the Cognitive Sciences of Music (17-22 August 2015) (656-660). Manchester: Royal Northern College of Music.

Pfefferle, D. and Fischer, J. (2006). "Sounds and size: identification of acoustic variables that reflect body size in hamadryas baboons, Papio hamadryas". In: *Animal Behavior*, 72, 43-51.

Pike, K. L. (1945). *The Intonation of American English*. Ann Arbor: University of Michigan Press.

Pinker, S. (1994). *The Language Instinct*. New York: Harper Perennial Modern Classics.

Plomp, R. and Levelt, W. J. M. (1965). "Tonal Consonance and Critical Bandwidth". In: *Journal of Acoustical Society of America*, 38, 548-560.

Plomp, R. and Steeneken, H. J. M. (1968). "Interference between two simple tones". In: *Journal of Acoustical Society of America*, 43, 883- 884.

Polka, L., Colantonio, C. and Sundara, M. (2001). "A cross-language comparison of /d/ to /ð/ perception: Evidence for a new developmental pattern". In: *Journal of the Acoustical Society of America*, 109(5), 2190-2201.

Preuschoft, S. and van Hooff, J. A. R. A. M. (1997). "The social function of "smile" and "laughter": variations across primate species and societies". In U. Segerstrale and P. Mobias, *Nonverbal Communication: Where Nature Meets Culture* (pp. 171-190). New Jersey: Lawrence Erlbaum Associates.

Provine, R. R. (2000). *Laughter: A Scientific Investigation*. New York: Viking Press.

Quinlan, P. T. (2002). "Evidence for the use of scene-based frames of reference in two-dimensional shape recognition". In C. W. Tyler (Ed.), *Human symmetry perception and its computational analysis* (pp. 85–109). Mahwah, NJ: Lawrence Erlbaum Associates.

Radocy, R. E. and Boyle, J. D. (1979). Psychological foundations of musical behavior. Springfield, IL: Charles C. Thomas Publisher, Ltd.

Raimondi, R. (1996). "Our problem is that everybody is 'deaf'". In: *EIR*, Vol. 23, No. 33, 32-33.

Ramachandran, V. S. and Hubbard, E. M. (2001). "Psychological investigations into the neural basis of synaesthesia". In: *Proceedings of the Royal Society*, 268, 979-983.

Rapoport, E. (1996). "Emotional expression code in opera and lied singing". In: *Journal of New Music Research*, 25(2), 109-149.

Redican, W. K. (1975). "Facial expressions in nonhuman primates". In L. Rosenblum (Ed.), *Primate Behavior: Developments in Field and Laboratory Research*, 4 (pp. 103-194). New York: Academic Press.

Ringeval, F., Chetouani, M. et al. (2008). "Automatic Prosodic Disorders Analysis for Impared Communication Children". Paper presented at the workshop on Child, Computer and Interaction. Chania, Greece.

Rollenhagen, J. E. and Olson, C. R. (2000). "Mirror image confusion in single neurons of macaque inferotemporal cortex". In: *Science*, 287, 1506–1508.

Rosen, D. (1995). *Verdi: Requiem*. Cambridge University Press.

Rosenfeld, L. (1988). "How the Nazis ruined musical tuning". In: *EIR*, Vol. 15, No. 35, 54.

Ross, M. D., Owren, M. J., Zimmermann, E. (2009). "Reconstructing the evolution of laughter in great apes and humans". In: *Current Biology*, 19(13), 1106–1111.

Rousseau, J.-J. (1998). *Essay on the Origin of Languages and Writings Related to Music*. London: Dartmouth College.

Rudhyar, D. (1922). "The Relativity of our Musical Conceptions". In: *Musical Quarterly*, 8 (January), 108-118.

Rummer, R., Schweppe, J., Schlegelmilch, R., Grice, M. (2014). "Mood is linked to vowel type: The role of articulatory movements". In: *Emotion*, 14(2): 246-250. doi: 10.1037/a0035752

Rushton, J. P., Vernon, P. A. and Bons, T. A. (2007). "No evidence that polymorphisms of brain regulator genes Microcephalin and ASPM are associated with general mental ability, head circumference or altruism". In: *Biology Letters*, 3, 157-160.

Saffran, J. R., Reeck, K., Niebuhr, A. and Wilson D. (2005). "Relative Pitch Changing the tune: the structure of the input affects infants' use of absolute and relative pitch". In: *Developmental Science*, 8(1), 1-7.

Salimpoor, V. N., Bosch, I. van den, Kovacevic, N., McIntosh, A. R., Dagher, A., Zatorre, R. J. (2013). "Interactions between the nucleus accumbens and auditory cortices predict music reward value". In: *Science*, Vol. 340, No. 6129, 216-219.

Sapir, E. (1929). "A Study in Phonetic Symbolism". In: *Journal of Experimental Psychology*, 12, 225-239.

Saussure, F. de (1966). *Course in General Linguistics.* C. Bally and A. Sechehaye (eds). New York: McGraw-Hill Book Company.

Scamvougeras, A., Kigar, D. L., Jones, D., Weinberger, D. R. and Witelson, S. F. (2003). "Size of the human corpus callosum is genetically determined: An MRI study in mono and dizygotic twins". In: *Neuroscience Letters*, 338, 91-94.

Schellenberg, E. G. and Trehub, S. E. (1996). "Natural musical intervals: Evidence from infant listeners". In: *Psychological Science*, 7(5), 272-277.

Scherer, K. R. and Oshinsky, J. S. (1977). "Cue Utilization in Emotion Attribution from Auditory Stimuli". In: *Motivation and Emotion*, 1(4), 331-346.

Scherer, K. R. (1981). "Speech and emotional states". In J. Darby, *Speech evaluation in psychiatry* (pp. 189-220). New York: Grune & Stratton.

Scherer, K. R. (1986). "Vocal affect expression: a review and a model for future research". In: *Psychological Bulletin*, 99, 143-165.

Schlosberg, H. (1954). "Three dimensions of emotion". In: *Psychological Review*, 61(2), 91-88.

Schneider, A. (2001). "Sound, pitch, and scale: From 'tone measurements' to sonological analysis in ethnomusicology". In: *Ethnomusicology*, 45 (3), 489–519.

Sergeant, D. (1969). "Experimental investigation of absolute pitch". In: *Journal of Research in Music Education*, 17, 135-143.

Sergeant, D. and Vraka, M. (2014). "Pitch perception and absolute pitch in advanced performers". In: I. Papageorgi and G. Welch (Eds.), *Advanced Musical Performance: Investigations in Higher Education Learning* (pp.201-231). Ashgate Publishing Limited.

Sergent, J., Ohta, S., MacDonald, B. (1992). "Functional neuroanatomy of face and object processing: a positron emission tomography study". In: *Brain*, 115, 15–36.

Shankweiler, D., Strange, W., & Verbrugge, R. (1977). Speech and the problem of perceptual constancy. In: Shaw R., & Bransford J. (Ed.), *Perceiving, acting, and knowing: Toward an ecological psychology* (pp. 315-345). New York: Erlbaum.

Sharon, R. and Walker, R. (2004). "A Typology of consonant agreement as correspondence". In: *Language*, 80, 475-531.

Shaw, G. M. (1878). "How sound and words are produced". In: *Popular Science Monthly*, Vol. 13, 43-53.

Simner, J., Ward, J., Lanz, M., Jansari, A., Noonan, K., Glover, L. and Oakley, D. A. (2005). "Non-random associations of graphemes to colours in synaesthetic and non-synaesthetic populations". In: *Cognitive Neuropsychology*, 22.8, 1069 - 1085.

Simner, J. (2006). "Beyond perception: synaesthesia as a psycholingual phenomenon". In: *Trends in Cognitive Sciences*, 11.1, 23 - 29.

Simner, J. and Hubbard, E. M. (2006). "Variants of synesthesia interact in cognitive tasks: Evidence for implicit associations and late connectivity in cross-talk theories". In: *Neuroscience*, 143, 805-814.

Sloboda, J. (1991). "Music Structure and Emotional Response: Some Empirical Finding". In: *Psychology of Music*, 19, 110-120.

Smith, D. R. R., Patterson, R. D., Turner, R., Kawahara, H., Irino, T. (2005). "The processing and perception of size information in speech sounds". In: *Journal of the Acoustical Society of America*, 117, 305-318.

Spencer, H. (1855). *Principles of Psychology*, Third edition, Vol 2. New York: Appleton.

Steinbeis, N., Koelsch, S., Sloboda, J., (2006). "The role of harmonic expectancy violations in musical emotions: evidence from subjective, physiological, and neural responses". In: *Journal of Cognitive Neuroscience*, 18 (8), 1380–1393.

Steinschneider, M., Volkov, I., Noh, D., Garell, P. and Howard, M. (1999). "Temporal encoding of voice onset time phonetic parameter by field potentials recorded directly from the human auditory cortex". In: *Journal of Neurophysiology*, 82(5), 2346–2357.

Stemple, J. C., Stanley, J., Lee, L. (1995). "Objective measures of voice production in normal subjects following prolonged voice use". In: *Journal of Voice*, 9, 127–133.

Stevens, J. (1986). *Words and Music in the Middle Ages: Song, Narrative, Dance and Drama, 1050-1350*. Cambridge: Cambridge University Press.

Stevens, K. N. (1998). *Acoustic Phonetics*. Cambridge, MA: The MIT Press.

Stevens, S. T. and Arieh, Y. (2005). "What you see is what you hear: The effect of auditory pitch on the detection of visual targets". Poster presented at the 76th annual meeting of the Eastern Psychological Society. Boston, MA.

Strange, W. (1989). "Dynamic specification of coarticulated vowels spoken in sentence context". In: *Journal of the Acoustical Society of America*, 85, 2135-2153.

Stratton, V. N. and Zalanowski, A. H. (1989). "The effects of music and paintings on mood". In: *Journal of Music Therapy*, 26, 30-41.

Stucchi, N., Graciô, V., Toneatto, C. and Scocchi, L. (2010). "The perceptual salience of symmetrical and asymmetrical sections of a line". In: *Perception*, 39, 1026–1042.

Stumpf, C. (2012). *The Origins of Music*. Oxford University Press.

Sugimoto, T., Kobayashi, H., Nobuyoshi, N., Kiriyama, Y., Takeshita, H., Nakamura, T. and Hashiya, K. (2010). "Preference for consonant music over dissonant music by an infant chimpanzee". In: *Primates*, 51, 7–12.

Sugiura, H., Masataka, N. (1995). "Temporal and acoustic flexibility in vocal exchanges of coo calls in Japanese macaques (Macaca fuscata)". In E. Zimmermann, J. D. Newman and U. Jurgen (pp. 121-140). New York: Plenum.

Sullivan, M. W., Lewis, M. (2003). "Contextual determinants of anger and other negative expressions in young infants". In: *Developmental Psychology*, 39, 693–705.

Sundberg, J. (1982). Speech, song and emotions. In: M. Clynes (Ed.), *Music, Mind and Brain: Neuropsychology of Music* (pp.137-149). New York: Plenum Press.

Sundberg, J. (1987). *The science of the singing voice*. DeKalb, IL: Northern Illinois University Press.

Sundberg, J, Lã, F. and Himonides, E. (2013). "Intonation and expressivity: a single case study of classical western singing". In: *Journal of Voice*, vol 27, no. 3, 391.e1-391.e8.

Swaddle, J. P. (1999). "Visual signaling by asymmetry: a review of perceptual processes". In: *Philosophical Transactions of the Royal Society of London B*, 354, 1383-1393.

Syrdal, A. K., & Gopal, H. S. (1986). "A perceptual model of vowel recognition based on the auditory represenation of American English vowels". In: *Journal of the Acoustical Society of America*, 79, 1086-1100.

Szameitat, D. P., Alter, K., Szameitat, J. A., Wildgruber, D., Sterr, A., Darwin, C. J. (2009). "Acoustic profiles of distinct emotional expressions in laughter". In: *Journal of Acoustical Society of America*, 126(1), 1-14.

Szameitat, D. P., Alter, K., Szameitat, A. J., et al. (2009). "Differentiation of emotions in laughter at the behavioral level". In: *Emotion*, 9, 397-405.

Takeuchi, A. H. and Hulse, S. H. (1993). "Absolute pitch". In: *Psychological Bulletin*, 113, 345– 361.

Tarte, R. D. (1981). "The relationship between monosyllables and pure tones: An investigation of phonetic symbolism". In: *Journal of Verbal Learning and Verbal Behaviour*, 21, 352-360.

Tartter, V. C. and Braun, D. (1994). "Hearing smiles and frowns in normal and whisper registers". In: *Journal of the Acoustical Society of America*, 96, 2101-2107.

Temperley, D. (2001). *The Cognition of Basic Musical Structures.* Cambridge MA: MIT Press.

Terhardt, E. (1968). "Uber akustische Rauhigkeit und Schwankungsstarke". In: *Acustica*, 20, 215- 224.

Terhardt, E. (1974). "Pitch, consonance and harmony". In: *Journal of Acoustical Society of America*, Vol. 55, No. 5, 1061-1069.

Terhardt, E. (1977). "The two-componentheory of musical consonance". In E. F. Evans and J. P. Wilson (Eds.), *Psychophysics and physiology of hearing*. London: Academic Press.

Tervaniemi, M., Kujala, A., Alho, K., Virtanen, J., Ilmoniemi, R. J., Näätänen, R. (1999). "Functional specialization of the human auditory cortex in processing phonetic and musical sounds: a magnetoencephalographic (MEG) study". In: *Neuroimage*, 9(3), 330–336.

Thompson, P. M., Cannon, T. D., Narr, K. L., Erp, T. van et al (2001). "Genetic influences on brain structure". In: *Nature Neuroscience*, 4, 1253-1258.

Tillmann, B., Janata, P., Bharucha, J. (2003). "Activation of the inferior frontal cortex in musical priming". In: *Cognitive Brain Research*, 16, 145–161.

Ting, Tan, Y., McPherson, G. E., Peretz, I., Berkovic, S. F., Wilson, S. J. (2014). "The genetic basis of music ability". In: *Frontiers in Psychology*, 5, 658.

Titze, I. R. (1989). "Physiological and acoustic differences between male and female voices". In: *Journal of the Acoustical Society of America*, 85, 1699-1707.

Tongeren, van M. C. (2002). *Overtone singing: Physics and metaphysics of harmonics in east and west*. Amsterdam: Fusica.

Traill, A. (1994). *A !Xoo Dictionary*. Koeln: Ruediger Koeppe Verlag.

Traunmüller, H. (2003). "Clicks and the idea of a human protolanguage". In: *PHONUM*, 9, 1-4.

Trehub, S. E., Schellenberg, E. G. and Nakata, T. (2008). "Cross-cultural perspectives on pitch memory". In: *Journal of Experimental Child Psychology*, 100, 40-52.

Treitler, L. (2003). *With Pen and Voice: Coming to know medieval song and how it was made*. New York: Oxford University Press.

Trubetzkoy, N. (1969). *Principles of phonology*. Translated by C. A. M. Baltaxe. Berkeley and Los Angeles: University of California Press.

Tsur, R. (2006). "Size-sound symbolism revisited". In: *Journal of Pragmatics*, 38, 905-924.

Ultan, R. (1978). "Size-Sound Symbolism". In Greenberg (Ed.), *Universals of Human Language* (pp. 525-568). Stanford, California: University Press.

Vago, R. M. (1976). "Theoretical implications of Hungarian vowel harmony". In: *Linguistic Inquiry*, 7, 243-263.

Vigotski, L. S. (1986). *Thought and Language*. A. Kozulin (rev. and ed). Cambridge MA: MIT Press.

Vlasenko, B., Philippou-Hubner, D., Prylipko, D., Bock, R., Siegert, I., and Wendemuth, A. (2011). "Vowels formants analysis allows straight forward detection of high arousal emotions". In: *Proceedings of the IEEE International Conference on Multimedia and Expo (ICME)*, Barcelona, Spain.

Vollaerts, J. W. A. (1958). *Rhythmic Proportions in Early Medieval Ecclesiastical Chant*. Leiden: E.J. Brill.

Vraka, M. (2010). *The influence of culture on the development of absolute pitch*. (PhD Thesis). London University, Institute of London.

Walker, R. (1990). *Music Beliefs – Mythical and Psychoacoustic Perspectives*. New York.

Ward, W. D. (1999). "Absolute pitch". In D. Deutsch (Ed.), *The psychology of music* (2nd ed., pp 265-298). San Diego, CA: Academic Press.

Ward, J. et al (2005). "A comparison of lexical-gustatory and grapheme-colour synaesthesia". In: *Cognitive Neuropsychology*, 22, 28-41.

Watt, H. J. (1917). *The psychology of sound*. London: Cambridge University Press.

Welch, G. (2005). "Singing as communication". In: D. Miell, R. MacDonald and D. J. Hargreaves (Eds.), *Musical Communication*, (pp.239-259). New York: Oxford University Press.

Welch, G. (2006). "Singing and Vocal Development". In: *The Child as Musician: a handbook of musical development* (pp. 311-329).

Welch, G., Himonides, E., Saunders, J., Papageorgi, I., Preti, C, Rinta, T., Vraka, M., Stephens Himonides, C., Stewart, C., Lanipekun, J. and

Hill, J. (2010). *Researching the impact of National Singing Programme "Sing Up" in England: Main findings from the first three years (2007-2010). Children's singing development, self-concept and sense of social inclusion.* London: International Music Education Research Centre, Institute of Education.

Wheeler, R. H. (1920). *The Synaesthesia of a Blind Subject.* Eugene, Oregon: Universitz of Oregon Press.

Wong, C., Law, K,. and Wong, P. (2004). "Development and validation of a forced choice emotional intelligence measure for Chinese respondents in Hong Kong". In: *Asia Pacific Journal of Management*, 21 (4), 535–559.

Woods, R. P., Freimer, N. B., De Young, J. A. et al (2006). "Normal variants of Microcephalin and ASPM do not account for brain size variability". In: *Human Molecular Genetics*, 15, 2025-2029.

Wright, A. A., Rivera, J. J., Hulse, S. H., Shyan, M. and Neiworth, J. J. (2000). "Music perception and octave generalization in rhesus monkeys". In: *Journal of Experimental Psychology: General*, 129, 291–307.

Wright, I. C., Sham, P., Murray, R. M. et al (2002). "Genetic contributions to regional variability in human brain structure: Methods and preliminary results". In: *NeuroImage*, 17, 256-271.

Xu, Y. and Chuenwattanapranithi, S. (2007). "Perceiving anger and joy in speech through the size code". In: *Proceedings of the 16th International Congress of Phonetic Sciences*, August 6-10, Saarbrucken, Germany, pp. 2105-2108.

Yildirim, N. et al. (1991). "The effect of posture on upper airway dimensions in normal subjects and in patients with the sleep apnea/hypopnea syndrome". In: *American Review of Respiratory Disease*, 144(4), 845-847.

Yildirim, M., Bulut, C. Lee, Kazemzadeh, Busso, C., Deng, Z., Lee, S. and Narayanan, S. (2004). "An acoustic study of emotions expressed". In: *Proceedings of the 8th International Conference on Spoken Language Processing*, Jeju island, Korea.

Zatorre, R. J., Halpern, A. R., Perry, D. W., Meyer, E., Evans, A. C. (1996). "Hearing in the mind's ear: a PET investigation of musical imagery and perception". In: *Journal for* Cognitive Neuroscience, 8, 29–46.

Zatorre, R. J., Belin, P. and Penhune, V. B. (2002). "Structure and function of auditory cortex: music and speech". In: *Trends in Cognitive Sciences*, 6 (1), 37-46.

Zatorre, R. J. (2003). "Absolute pitch: A model for understanding the influence of genes and development on neural and cognitive function". In: *Nature Neuroscience*, 6, 692-695.

Zeitlin, L. R. (1964). "Frequency Discrimination of pure and complex tones". In: *Journal of the Acoustical Society of America*, 36, 1207.

www.ingramcontent.com/pod-product-compliance
Lightning Source LLC
Chambersburg PA
CBHW070546090426
42735CB00013B/3084